THE PSALMS

THE PSALMS

A New Translation

BONAVENTURE ZERR, O. S. B.

PAULIST PRESS
New York/Ramsey/Toronto

Nihil Obstat:
+Most Reverend Kenneth Steiner
Censor Deputatis

Imprimatur:
+Most Reverend Cornelius M. Power
Archbishop of Portland

December 5, 1978

Library of Congress
Catalog Card Number:
79-53694

ISBN: 0-8091-2218-9

Published by Paulist Press
Editorial Office
1865 Broadway, New York, N.Y. 10023
Business Office
545 Island Road, Ramsey, N.J. 07446

Printed and bound in the
United States of America

*Dedicated to the memory of
Abbot Damian Jentges, O.S.B.
without whom this translation
would never have come about*

Acknowledgements

A work such as the present translation, done by a Benedictine monk, living in a community of Benedictine monks, is not the product of a single person. So much help of every kind has gone into the production of this work by my confreres that I seriously considered placing "The Monks of Mount Angel Abbey" as the authors. In some ways, this would be a more true representation of the facts than the wording that is given on the title page. Yet the basic work of rendering the Hebrew original into English is mine, and so these lines are added to explain that, while my name appears, others deserve much credit.

This translation was not my idea to begin with. Nine years ago, my confreres were attempting to produce liturgical texts for public prayer, when I arrived home from Europe. I was invited to participate in this work, and the psalms happened to be my special area of study and interest. A full and new translation of the psalms was the result. The present version offered here represents a second revision of that original, which was privately printed, and which has been used in the public prayer of Mount Angel Abbey since 1973.

During the course of the original translating and the later revisings, many of the brethen contributed invaluably to the work. I especially wish to mention Father Bruno Becker, O.S.B. Some of the phrases in this work which I consider to be the best are in reality his. Many valuable suggestions were offered by Abbot Anselm Galvin. Much of the typing was done by Father Augustine DeNoble, O.S.B., and most of the typing of the present manuscript was done by Brother Brian Clearman, O.S.B., who also proved to be a driving spirit in bringing this work forth. Also deserving of mention are Father Joel Kehoe, O.S.B. and Brother Konrad Schaefer, O.S.B. who acted as proofreaders. And much of the help and support for this project was given in that quiet sort of way that is characteristic of the best elements in a monastery's life. May the Father, who sees in secret, reward all who have aided in finishing this work.

Preface

"Every translator is a traitor"—so runs a much used and ancient bromide. There is much truth in the proverb for no translation can ever do justice to the original language. The ancient savant who rendered the Book of Sirach into Greek was aware of the problem, and made the added point that there is a particular poignancy to the translator's difficulty when Hebrew is the language with which one begins.

In the course of working on this translation that has been a project of several years' duration, the translator has had occasion to feel himself in agreement with the grandson of Jesus ben Sirach. Nor is it merely the peculiar eloquence of Hebrew poetry that is the cause of the translator's task being hard; there is the fact that recent discoveries which shed much bright light on former obscurities of Hebrew grammar and offer much to augment even the best of our old lexicons at the same time cause much havoc by challenging received knowledge of the language and leaving the would-be student with more questions than answers about how to translate many passages.

In addition to this the contemporary translator of the psalms is faced with many other challenges from the greatly expanded knowledge we now possess about the thought world and cultural milieu of ancient Israel. In other words, one is nowadays called upon to render boldly many lines of the psalter in the light of what is now known of ancient Israelite thinking. These translations are bound to strike as daring and even dubious the ears of anyone who is used to the more traditional versions. In this regard, a few words of explanation seem helpful and even necessary.

Our received knowledge and understanding of the Hebrew language was largely collated and formulated by Jewish scholars several centuries after Christ. Few others paid much mind to the Hebrew language which by that time had become (except among Jews) a dead language. We owe a great deal to those Jewish scholars, for their work was as remarkable as it was exacting and careful. But in the field of linguistics and historical research of their own language, they were actually in possession of less machinery than is our present age. Moreover, their religious awareness had been conditioned by the evolution of their own religion and its teaching.

The psalms had come to birth, by and large, anywhere from six hundred to one thousand years before the Jewish scholars under discussion did their work. This means that these splendid poems were composed in a world that still used the language of myth and mythopoesis as the primary means of religious communication and were written in a living Hebrew closely related to other dialects of the Northwest Semitic branch of the Semitic language family.

The modern student of the psalms must take these vital facts into careful consideration. Words, expressions, and idioms which came to have one meaning for the rabbis of, say, 500 A.D., may well have enjoyed very different meanings or nuances for the Israel of 700 B.C. Recent discoveries, particularly in the field of Ugaritic and other Northwest Semitic languages, enable us to come much closer in time and thought to the original feelings and ways of speech of the ancient Israelite than scholars of the post-Christian era could, no matter how careful and diligent their work may have been.

Moreover, great strides have been made in understanding the thought world of ancient Israel. We are presently in a much better position to evaluate the religious picture of pre-exilic Israel than our forefathers were, and we are much closer to understanding the historical development of the Israelite religion than men of even a generation or so past. For understanding the message and the poetry of the psalms and for translating them into meaningful English this fact is very important.

The mythology which the authors of the psalms employed is a case in point. It has become clearer to all who study the matter nowadays that the Israelites formulated their Yahwist religion in the thought patterns and myths of the peoples around them, chiefly the Canaanites. The original formulation and understanding of their monotheism was made possibly in the desert and for desert conditions. Settlement of the land, the transition from nomadic to agricultural living and ultimately to a high degree of urbanization—all of these factors necessitated a concomitant development of Israel's religious life. Just as Israel borrowed heavily from her new neighbors in Palestine their cultural forms, so did she learn to express her faith in their modes and idioms. It might be remarked that this was not a process free of dangers and excesses; and psalmist as well as prophet, not to mention many passages of the Law, had frequently to separate sheep from goats among the ardent admirers of the superior Canaanite civilization.

Still, Israel found much she could use in the mythical language of Canaan. Thus, the psalms frequently conceive of Yahweh in the trappings of the Canaanite chief god, El. El reigns over a whole circle of gods, and, while his authority among them is supreme, they are an unruly lot and there are frequent quarrels among them in the Canaanite myths. Famous and important among these fights is the perpetual hostility between Baal, god of life and fertility, who annually brings rain to the land, against Mot, god of death and lord of the world below. Ancient myths seem to have viewed the annual summer dry spell as a period when Mot was in the ascendency; the subsequent rainy season and new birth of nature was Baal's element.

Connected with the theme of life and death in nature and using the same or similar vocabularly was the frequent theme of Israel's thinking of the life and death of man. There is much talk in the psalms about death and the realm where the death-god, Mot, held sway. His domain goes by many names in the Hebrew psalter: "the world below," "the Pit," "the place of decay," "the city of death," along with much else that is descriptive. (It might be added that the rabbis of old often missed the nuances of these names and assigned other meanings to expressions for death's domains.)

In Israelite poetry the functions of gods who were benign, like Baal and El, are performed by Yahweh, who alone is God. Yahweh is thus spoken of as the Creator—but not as a Christian theologian of the 13th century would have represented the Creator, as one who brings something from nothing; nor even, for that matter, as a contemporary follower of Teilhard de Chardin would have done. The psalmist speaks in the language of his own era, and hence creation is seen as Yahweh's victory over the forces of primeval chaos, the dark, unformed watery powers personified by Yam, the sea god. Creation was the suppression of Yam and his sinister minions, and the consequent ordering of all other powers under the sway of Yahweh's rule.

Since the primeval time when all that happened, Yahweh has constructed for himself a palace in the heavens (cf. Ps. 8). There he reigns supreme over the lower heavens and the earth and even under this earth, the nether-world, the world below, the realm of the dead. Color is added to this picture by surrounding Yahweh with the denizens of the Canaanite Pantheon, the lesser Canaanite gods, who are, of course, at Yahweh's beck and call. These deities are called the "Holy Ones" by the Canaanites, and were believed by them to take care of the governing of the earth. The psalms ridicule this latter notion (cf. Pss. 16, 58, 83) and emphasize that Yahweh is the Supreme Master and Ruler of the earth.

[xi]

This lordship of Yahweh is emphasized in certain royal psalms (i.e., psalms which probably had their origin in court circles and liturgies). In these Yahweh is addressed as the Suzerain or Sovereign over all, and Israel's king is his vassal. Lesser deities have nothing to say about government and the scheme of salvation which is in these psalms something between Yahweh and his Israelite vassal.

These are but a few of the considerations which lie behind this translation and the translator hopes eventually to publish a commentary that will fully explain why he has done what he has done. In the meantime this translation is offered in the hope that it will be of assistance first and foremost as a means of prayer to all who use it. The reader is referred to the many existing commentaries available. Among these a special mention must be made of the three-volume commentary by Father Mitchell Dahood, S.J., in the Anchor Bible.[1] The translator has relied heavily on Father Dahood's work in preparing this translation. Also deserving a special mention is the commentary of J. W. Rogerson and J. W. McKay[2] as well as the two-volume work by A. A. Anderson.[3]

One of the best of all my teachers once said that the rest of the Old Testament was the best commentary on the psalter and I heartily concur in this dictum. The reader is encouraged to penetrate ever more deeply into the Old Testament whereby he will enter the realm of the psalms more correctly, as well as understand the faiths of both Judaism and Christianity—neither of which could ever survive without the full acceptance of the Old Testament.

Bonaventure Zerr, O.S.B.
August 1, 1978

[1]Garden City, N. Y.: Doubleday, 1966-70; abbreviated in this work as PAB.
[2]Cambridge, The Cambridge University Press, 1977.
[3]London, Oliphants, 1972.

The Psalms

Psalm 1

Of Psalm 1 Saint Jerome said that it is " . . . the main entrance to the mansion of the psalter." It does seem to have been placed at the head of the collection as a sort of introduction. It may be a sort of wisdom poem, a meditation on the principal themes contained in the psalms. Perhaps it is based on an ancient Israelite liturgy of blessing and cursing. The wicked described by the psalm are probably men unfaithful to the Lord, idolaters of some kind. Their counsel attempts to lead faithful men from the instruction or law of Yahweh. They scoff at the trust of the faithful men and so are called the "scornful" in verse 1. But the road they travel leads ultimately to perdition.

1　Happy is the man who does not walk with the
　　　　wicked,
　　who does not stand with sinners
　　nor take his seat among the scornful.

2　He finds delight in the law of Yahweh;
　　he reflects on it night and day.

3　He is like a tree
　　planted beside streams full of water—
　　a tree that bears its fruit,
　　whose leaves will never fail.

　　In all that he does,
　　prosperity will attend him.

4　But the wicked are not like this.
　　They are like chaff, blown away by the wind.

5　At the judgment these will not take their stand;
　　sinners will not stand in the assembly of the just.

6　Yahweh takes care of the way of the just,
　　but the way of the wicked leads to ruin.

Psalm 2

This psalm is a poem used in the liturgy of installing the king in the Jerusalem monarchy. Perhaps this festival was an annual institution in Judah. The poem speaks as if the vassal kings, subject to the king in Jerusalem, were in revolt, a circumstance which frequently attended the interregnum. Since the Davidic monarch was regarded as the adopted son of God, it is the Lord himself who undertakes to put down the forlorn rebellion of the subject kinglets. Then he formally installs his own chosen king and promises him success in his reign. The psalm concludes with a warning to would-be upstarts and a blessing for those who recognize Yahweh's overlordship.

1 Why are the nations in turmoil?
   Why do the peoples devise their vain conspiracies?

2 The kings of the land rise in revolt;
   rulers conspire against Yahweh and his anointed.

3 "Let us break their bonds," they cry;
   "let us hurl their chains away!"

4 The One enthroned in heaven laughs;
   with contempt the Sovereign Lord regards them.

5 In anger he will address them
   and his fury will intimidate them.

6 Of me he says: "This is my king;
   I have enthroned him on Zion, my holy
          mountain."

7 Let me proclaim Yahweh's decree:
   "You are my Son," he said;
   "on this day I have become your father.

8 Ask me, and I shall make nations your heritage;
   all the land will be yours.

9 You will break them with an iron scepter,
   shattering them like a vessel of clay."

10 So now, kings, learn wisdom;
    rulers of the earth, take warning:

11 worship Yahweh with all reverence.

Mortal men, (12) pay him your homage,
so he will not be angry and you will not be lost,
for his anger can flare up in a moment.

How fortunate are all who take refuge in him.

Psalm 3

The speaker in this psalm may well have been an Israelite king. The Lord is addressed here as the protector of the psalmist and both the terms of distress and the requests for assistance are made in military language. Perhaps the original setting for the psalm was a liturgy in which the king or his spokesman called on Yahweh and was answered in an oracle with the assurance of victory over enemies and a blessing on the people.

1   *A psalm of David when he was in flight from Absalom, his son.*

2   How my enemies have multiplied, Yahweh!
     More and more rise up to oppose me.

3   About me many are saying:
     "God will give him no victory."

4   But you, Yahweh, are a shield to cover me;
     you are my Glory, and you hold up my head.

5   I cry aloud to Yahweh
     and he answers me from his holy mountain.

6   I can lie down and sleep, and then awake,
     for Yahweh sustains me.

7   I am not afraid of those tens of thousands
     who set on me from all sides.

8   Rise up, Yahweh, and save me, my God!
     Strike all my enemies across the face
     and break the teeth of the wicked![a]

9   O Yahweh, give victory!
     On your people be your blessing!

---

[a] The violence of this petition is somewhat mollified when we remember that it is but a request that the weapons of the enemies be rendered ineffective.

Psalm 4

A prayer for rain. Since the very existence of ancient Israel depended on an adequate rainfall each year, it was most vital that this precipitation be secured. The pagans surrounding Israel, and indeed dwelling in her midst, worshipped fertility gods and goddesses to obtain a good growing season and abundant crops. The Israelites loyal to the covenant countered with liturgies and prayers to Yahweh for the same purpose. The oracles and poems of the prophets assure us that there was a constant struggle even in the highest circles of Israel to maintain fidelity to Yahweh and that the focus of the contest was the ability of the heavenly powers to bestow the blessing of the rains (cf. 1 Kings 18). The present psalm reflects this controversy. It is a prayer of fidelity to the Lord which excoriates the "men of rank" and others who look to "worthless idols" to produce the great "blessing" which is the rainfall. Because of the confidence expressed in the psalm in terms of rest and sleep (terms which may originally have referred to some liturgical or ritual gesture) the Church has traditionally used this psalm as a night prayer. Its unswerving confidence in God does make this a fitting meditation at the end of each day.

1 *For the director: on stringed-instruments.*
   A psalm of David.

2 Answer me when I call to you.
   You are the God who gives me what is just.

   When I am in anguish,[a] release me;
   have mercy and hear my prayer.

3 How long will you men of rank dishonor my God
      of glory?
   How long will you love worthless idols
   and consult oracles that lie?

---

a This "anguish" in the Hebrew is called "the siege", for the forces of Death
  and his ally, drought, are besieging the holy land.

4 Know that Yahweh works wonders
  for those who are devoted to him.
  Yahweh hears me whenever I call him.

5 Fear him, and sin no more;
  on your beds,^b reflect and be still.

6 Offer sacrifices that are fitting.
  and put your trust in Yahweh.

7 "Who will bring us blessing?" many are asking.
  "The light of your face has fled from us,
      Yahweh."^c

8 Give a joy to my heart,
  greater than men have from their gods of grain
      and wine.

9 I will lie down in peace,
  and sleep will come at once,
  for you alone, Yahweh, make me live in
      prosperity.

---

^b The "beds" may be the equivalent of what today would be called "pews" or
this may be an idiom referring to the ideal place of prayer and meditation.
^c This expression reflects the fear of those of weak faith. Yahweh's favor has
deserted Israel, and thus the idols must be called to the rescue. Contrast this
with the psalmist's confidence in the next two verses.

Psalm 5

This psalm in which the poet proclaims his fidelity to Yahweh in the face of idol worship requests the blessing of life while stating the belief that idolatry has fatal consequences. It might be classed, rather loosely, as a psalm of innocence. The psalmist asks for the divine consideration, bringing his plea to the temple at first light. He presents his case, which can be assumed by implication to be his claim to innocence of involvement in idol worship. He asks for rescue from his idolatrous opponents, stating his belief that the blandishments of these men lead to death and reminding Yahweh of the rewards promised to men loyal to the covenant.

1   *For the director: for the wind instruments.*
    A psalm of David.

2   Listen to my words, Yahweh;
    consider what I say.

3   Heed my cry for help, my King and my God.
    because it is to you that I pray, (4) Yahweh.

    In the morning you will listen to my voice;
    in the morning I will present my cause and watch
        for you.

5   Evil would please only a false god;
    as for you, no sinner can be a guest of yours,

6   the boastful cannot stand before your face.

7   You hate all who worship idols
    and you destroy those who proclaim deceit.
    Yahweh abhors those who worship idols and false
        gods.

8   But through your great love I will enter your
        house.
    I will bow low toward your holy temple
    in reverence for you, (9) Yahweh.

Lead me into your Meadow of Life[a]
because my enemies are lurking for me.
Give me a level way to follow.

10 What comes from their mouths cannot be trusted;
destruction is in their hearts,
their throats are open graves,
their tongues bring death.[b]

11 Bring them to an end, O God;
let them fall by their own intrigues.
Cast them down, after all their rebellions,
because they have defied you.

12 But joy to all who take refuge in you!
Let them sing out for joy.
You are the shelter of those who love your name
so they may rejoice in you.

13 Indeed, it is you that will bless
the man of virtue, Yahweh;
your favor is a shield that covers him.

---

[a] Fr. Dahood (PAB, I, pp. 33-34) suggests this translation. More traditionally,
this line is usually rendered: "Lead me into your righteousness!", but
Dahood is probably correct in his translation. The phrase need not mean,
however, as he maintains, that the psalmist is praying for entrance into
heaven. He may be using mythical language to pray for prosperity.

[b] The idol worshippers here described are endowed by the psalmist as very like
Mot, the Canaanite deity of death. Unwittingly, they are Mot's allies as they
seek to entice God's people away from him who is the source of all life.

Psalm 6

This psalm appears to be the prayer of a sick man, but it has the overtones of a song which protests idolatry. The psalmist begs for release from sickness and death, describes his plight, and finally drives from him the idol worshippers who would entice him to seek favor of false gods, inviting them to depart into the Land of the Lost, that is, the realm of the dead, which is the proper habitation of dead gods.

1   *For the directors: for strings: on the eighth.*
    A psalm of David.

2   Do not convict me in your anger, Yahweh;
    do not punish me in your wrath.

3   Have compassion on me, Yahweh, because I am
        ill.
    Heal me, Yahweh, because my very bones are
        aching

4   and my throat is throbbing!

    And you, O Yahweh—how long?

5   Yahweh, relent and rescue me:
    save me—your kind love demands it.

6   Certainly in the land of the dead
    there is no remembrance of you.[a]
    Who sings your praises in Sheol?

7   I am worn out from sobbing.
    Every night my pillow is wet with my tears,
    and my bed is drenched with my crying.

8   My vision is blurred with sorrow;
    my heart grows old from grief.

---

[a] The lack of remembrance spoken of here does not mean loss of memory. Expressions such as this in the psalms deal with the belief that in Sheol, the realm of the dead, there are no liturgical celebrations of Yahweh. Perhaps here the psalmist is reminding the Lord that while he is ill and hence in a sense in Sheol, he cannot partake in temple worship.

9 Leave me, all you worshippers of idols,
    it is Yahweh who hears the sound of my
        weeping.

10 It is Yahweh who listens to my pleading for
        favor;
    it is Yahweh who accepts my prayer.

11 Let all my enemies feel shame and terror;
    let them all go back in shame
    to the Land of the Lost.

Psalm 7

This poem is a lament, perhaps originally made by some public official or even a king. The psalmist begs the assistance of Yahweh. He takes a strongly worded oath to protest his fidelity to the covenant, his innocence of association with idols, and then prays for the final judgment of Yahweh. Finally he returns to the theme of his adversaries, idolaters doing death's own work, and concludes with a declaration of his intention to remain faithful in worshipping the Lord.

1   *An impassioned lament of David, which he sang to Yahweh after the declarations of Cush, the Benjaminite.*

2   Yahweh, my God, I take refuge with you.
    Save me from all my pursuers;

3   rescue me or they will tear me to pieces,
    like lions at my neck they will mangle me
    and no one will rescue me.

4   Yahweh, my God, if I have committed an outrage,[a]
    if guilt clings to my palms;

5   if I have repaid my covenant partner[b] with evil,
    or if I have yielded to my adversaries, the worthless idols:

6   then let my Enemy[c] come after me and overtake me!
    Let him trample my life into the world below!
    Let him stomp my very body into the Mud.[d]

---

a   The "outrage" and "guilt" to which the psalmist refers are acts of idolatry of which he declares himself innocent.
b   The covenant partner is possibly Yahweh himself.
c   The "Enemy" is Death, who often in the psalter is spoken of as *the* Enemy, *par excellence.*
d   The Mud is a poetic name for the nether-world, the realm of death.

7   Rise up in your anger, Yahweh;
    rouse yourself against the presumption of my
          enemies;
    Awake, my God! Order justice done!

8   Let the nations assemble around you.
    O Most High, take your throne above them.

9   Yahweh, pass sentence on the peoples.
    Judge me, Yahweh, according to my virtue,
    according to my innocence, O Most High.

10 Take vengeance on the evil of the impious,
    and confirm the position of the virtuous.
    The one who appraises both mind and heart
    is God the Just One.

11 God, the Most High, is the shield that protects
          me,
    and he preserves men with upright hearts.

12 God is a judge who is just;
    he vindicates his rights every day.

13 If only the Conqueror would sharpen his sword;
    if only he would bend his bow and make it ready,

14 prepare deadly shafts
    and tip his arrows with fire!

15 But my adversary is in labor with wickedness;
    he is conceiving evil and giving birth to lies.

16 He is digging a pit—may it be his undoing!
    May he fall into the trap he is constructing.

17 May his malice recoil upon his own head;
    may his violence fall upon himself!

18 I will thank Yahweh for his justice;
    I will sing hymns to the name of Yahweh, the
          Most High.

Psalm 8

This psalm is a hymn which praises the Lord as Creator, recalling the marvels of his creative work and emphasizing man as the crown of that work. The hymn begins and ends with a refrain, possibly to be sung by a choir, while the body of the song is sung by an individual. The motifs used suggest that the psalm was once used during the autumn festival which celebrated the creation.

1   *For the director: upon the gittith.*
    A psalm of David.

2   O Yahweh, our Sovereign,
        what awe your Name[a] inspires through all the
            earth!
    I will worship your glory beyond the heavens,

3   though my words are the sound
        of infants and babes.
    You established a stronghold against your enemies
    after you subdued the foe and the avenger.[b]

4   When I look up at the heavens,
        the work of your fingers,
    at the moon and the stars
        which you set in their places,

5   what is man that you should provide for him,
        that mere mortal, that you watch over him?

6   Yet you made him nearly a god,
        crowning him with glory and honor;

---

a   The "Name" of God is an expression denoting his presence, especially the presence of his power and providence.

b   In the oldest Israelite accounts of creation, God is presented as having fought the powers of chaos (here referred to under the names "foe" and "avenger." His victory gained, the Lord constructed a heavenly palace from which he governs the universe.

7 you gave him dominion over the works of your
     hands.
   You put all things under his feet:

8 large animals and small—all of them,
   even the wild beasts and (9) the birds in the air
   and the fish that make their way
   along the paths of the seas.

10 O Yahweh, our Sovereign,
   what awe your name inspires through all the
   earth!

Psalm 9 (9A)

The controversy as to whether Psalms 9 and 10 are one psalm or two is one of the most ancient of all disputes about the psalter. The present Hebrew text has opted for the two-psalm theory. But it seems that the two are actually a single unit. Critics of this theory point to the hymnic character of Psalm 9 and the elements of lament contained in Psalm 10. But actually divergences of just this sort are not rare in the psalter; Psalms 27, 40, and 89 are characterized by similar discrepancies. Psalm 9 begins with a hymn of thanks to God, probably by someone who speaks for the whole worshipping community. Yahweh has acted on behalf of the nation before. Now he is asked with confidence to extend his saving actions on the part of the Zion community.

1 *For the director: according to Muth Labben.*
   A psalm of David.

2 I will thank you, Yahweh, with all my heart;
   I will retell all your wonders.

3 I will be glad and rejoice because of you.

4 I will sing hymns to your name, O Most High,
   when my enemies are turned back,
   when they stumble and perish at the sight of you!

5 If only you would take up my judgment and my
        case;
   if only you would take your place
   on your throne, Just Judge!

6 Issue a rebuke to the nations!
   Annihilate the wicked!
   Erase their names forever and beyond!

7 May the foe come to an end,
   like desolate ruins, forever!
   Destroy their protecting gods!
   and let all worship of them be forgotten!

8 But Yahweh—
from all eternity he has sat enthroned.
He has placed his throne for the judgment.

9 He is the one who rules the world with justice;
he judges the peoples with equity.

10 Truly, Yahweh is a stronghold for the
downtrodden,
a stronghold in times of distress.

11 Those who treasure your name may well trust in
you;
you do not abandon those who care for you,
Yahweh.

12 Sing hymns to Yahweh, who dwells on Zion;
relate his deeds among the peoples.

13 He cares for those who mourn,
and remembers their lament;
he does not forget the poor and their cry for help.

14 Have pity on me, Yahweh!
Look at the affliction brought on me by my
Enemy.

15 Bring me back from the gates of Death,
that I may recount your praises,
that I may dance and sing of your victory
at the gates of Daughter Zion.

16 May the nations be trapped
in the pit they have made,
their feet caught in the snare they have set.

17 May Yahweh be known for his judgment.
May the wicked man be ensnared
by the work of his own hands,

18 and go down among the dead.
May the nations perish if they forget God.

19 May the destitute not be forgotten forever,
nor the hope of the poor be always in vain.

20 Arise, Yahweh!
Let men not prevail!
Let the nations be brought before you for
judgment!

21 Put a muzzle on them, Yahweh!
Let the nations know they are but mortal.

Psalm 10 (9B)

As noted in the heading to the previous psalm, Psalm 10 is probably but a continuation and intensification of Psalm 9. The present poem describes the works and pomps of the idolatrous man: unhampered by the social and moral consequences of the law of the Lord, he spreads his doctrine of "liberation" from the power of Yahweh (vv. 3-7) and proceeds to oppress his helpless victims (vv. 8-11). The psalmist calls on the Lord in desperate phrases and begs him to deliver the poor faithful who must suffer because of their loyalty to him.

1 Why, Yahweh, do you stand so far away?
Why do you conceal yourself in times of anguish?

2 Oppression is the smoldering desire of the sinner.
He longs to accomplish his schemes.

3 The wicked man boasts about his inmost desire;
his own greed is what the despoiler adores.

The wicked man scorns Yahweh;
4 he thinks the Lofty One will not follow through
with his anger,
that God will not upset his plans,
5 that his wealth will last for all time!

Exalted Lord, your judgments are far from him;
he scoffs at them with all his being.

6 In his heart, he says: "I will never stumble;
always I will be without misfortune, always
happy."

7 His mouth is filled with talk about lying idols
and oppression;
behind his words are trouble and worthless images.

8 He sits in ambush within the towns;
from his hiding-place he kills the innocent man.

His eyes are on the look-out for the unfortunate
man;

[20]

9   he lurks in his hiding-place like a lion in the
        jungle.

    He crouches to leap on the wretch,
    to pounce on him and drag him away.

10   He beats the oppressed into his net
    and the unfortunate fall into his pit.

11   In his heart, he says: "God has forgotten!
    He has turned his face away and will never look!"

12   Rise up, Yahweh God!
    Raise your hand!
    Do not forget the poor!

13   Why should the evil man scorn God
    and say in his heart: "He never punishes?"

14   See for yourself the suffering;
    look at the grief and take it in your own hand.

    On you the unfortunate and the fatherless
        have thrown themselves.
    Be their helper.

15   Break the power of the evil man!
    Refund his malice till you find it is gone.

16   Yahweh is King to eternity and beyond!
    Let the nations be deported from his land!

17   Yahweh, listen to the desire of the poor.
    Let your heart be attentive and your ears alert.

18   Judge the fatherless and the oppressed.
    Let the humble man never again be driven
        from the land.

Psalm 11 (10)

This psalm is the declaration, apparently public and perhaps by a public man such as a prophet, of trust in Yahweh and his providence. The faint-hearted, those tempted to put their faith in the high-places, the mountains where idols were worshipped (v. 1), are addressed by the psalmist, who affirms his confidence in Yahweh's rule over the world despite appearances. He concludes with a ringing declaration that Yahweh will punish the wicked and reward the just.

1 *For the director: of David.*

It is in Yahweh that I have taken refuge;
How can you tell me:
"Flee to the mountains like a bird!"[a]

2 See how the wicked are bending their bows;
they are fixing their arrows on the strings
to shoot from dark ambush[b] at the upright of
heart.

3 While the foundations are being demolished,
what is the Just One doing?"

4 In his heavenly palace is the holy place of
Yahweh;
beyond the sky is the throne of Yahweh.

He is watching carefully,
his gaze is fixed on the sons of men.

---

a Commentators have generally considered this line as a suggestion to the poet to run away to the hills for safety. But it may well be that the true meaning of this expression is that the psalmist is invited to take part in the pagan cults that were practiced on the high places and hills. For another example of this line of thinking, see Psalm 121:1. Psalm 84:4 mentions the birds dwelling at Yahweh's shrine.

b The expression "dark ambush" (literally "gloom") suggests that those who threaten the good are in league with the powers of darkness, i.e., the forces of death which dwell in "Gloomville," a poetic name for the nether-world.

5 Yahweh, the Just One, is on the watch for the
     wicked,
  with all his being he loathes the man who loves
     violence.[c]

6 He rains down on the wicked blazing lightning,
  sulphur and a scorching wind for their cup.

7 Truly, Yahweh is the Just One,
  he loves deeds that are just.
  He is the Upright One;
  we shall gaze upon him

[c] The "man who loves violence" seems to be a reference to men who in some
   form practice idolatry. Unhampered by the prescriptions of the law of the
   Lord, these men exercised "violence" on law-abiding Israelites through
   financial or other forms of oppression.

Psalm 12 (11)

This psalm is a lament used in a liturgy. Verses 1-5 pray for deliverance from the faithless, who are portrayed as false-hearted, boastful oppressors. There follows an oracle from the Lord, which is contrasted with the lying words of the oppressors. Finally there is a brief prayer for divine protection. Verse 9 is difficult and the translation is conjectural.

1 *For the director: upon "the eighth."*
   A psalm of David.

2 Rescue us, Yahweh,
   for there are no loyal men left.
   Men who are steadfast in faith have disappeared.

3 They lie to one another;
   they speak with deceitful lips and false hearts.

4 May Yahweh destroy deceitful lips,
   tongues that keep boasting,

5 those that say, "Our tongues make us strong,
   our lips are weapons for us; who is our master?"

6 Yahweh says: "Because of the sobbing of the poor
   and the sighing of the needy,
   now shall I arise.
   To anyone who longs for safety I shall give it."

7 The promises of Yahweh are promises without
      alloy:
   silver refined in a crucible and seven times purged
      of dross.

8 Yahweh, protect us!
   Guard us from this generation, Eternal One!

9 On every side the wicked are prowling,
   yes, perfidy is praised among the sons of men.

Psalm 13 (12)

This psalm is the lament of an individual. Though the circumstances of its composition or use are not entirely obvious, it seems that the Enemy that is feared is Death. Perhaps the psalm was meant to be the cry of a sick man. The four-fold repetition of the phrase "How long . . ." indicates the protracted nature of the suffering described, and the very sound of this repeated phrase in the Hebrew indicates the depth of the lament.

1   *For the director: a psalm of David.*

2   How long, O Yahweh?
    Will you go on forgetting me?
    How long are you going to hide your face
        from me?

3   How long will I have to suffer anguish in my soul,
    and bear sorrow in my heart night and day?
    How long will my enemy triumph over me?

4   Look and answer me, O Yahweh, my God.
    Give my eyes light, or I will sleep in death.

5   My Enemy will say: "I overcame him";
    my Foe will rejoice that I fell.[a]

6   But I trust in your unfailing love,
    my heart rejoices in your deliverance.

    I will sing to Yahweh:
    how good the Most High is to me!

a The "Enemy" and the "Foe" in this verse are one and the same: Death.

Psalm 14 (13)

This psalm is a lament, but it is reflective in the style of some wisdom poems. Somewhat in the style of Genesis 6, the psalmist describes the corruption of his own times. Though some of the translation of this psalm remains obscure, it seems clear that the psalmist expresses his conviction that the Lord remains on the side of his lowly faithful ones and will deliver them from the hardships they must suffer.

1   *For the director: a psalm of David.*

    The fool declares in his heart: "God has no
        power!"
    Men are depraved, they commit outrageous acts:
    not one does anything good.

2   Yahweh looks down from heaven upon all men
    to see if any are wise,
    if a single one is seeking God.

3   All are obstinate,
    all alike are corrupt.
    Not one does anything good,
    not a single one.

4   Those idolaters who devour his people—
    will they not understand?
    It is Yahweh's grain, which they did not gather,
    that they are devouring.

5   They have formed a conspiracy,
    but God is in the assembly of the virtuous.

6   The council of the lowly will defeat it,
    because Yahweh is their refuge.

7   If only Israel's deliverance would come out of
        Zion!
    When Yahweh gives a good harvest to his people,
    then will Jacob rejoice and Israel be glad.

Psalm 15 (14)

This psalm may have been used once as an examen for those about to participate in worship at a shrine. But it seems that the psalm contains more than just a list of do's and dont's for members of a congregation. The mention of the "tent" of Yahweh and his "holy mountain" suggests a more far-reaching concept of being a guest for the one who prayed this psalm. Perhaps a life is suggested which can form a spiritual communion with the Lord. The last verse of the psalm implies this: the man who lives by the precepts laid down in the body of the psalm is promised: he will not stumble ever. This "stumbling" is done by those who live in an evil way, under the influence of the forces of evil. The man who orders his life by these commands can walk in a way that is spiritually secure.

1 *A psalm of David.*

Yahweh, who can be a guest in your tent?
Who can dwell on your holy mountain?

2 It is the one who walks perfectly with you
and whose deeds are all according to your will;
the man whose heart speaks the truth
3 whose words will not trip him up;

the one who does no wrong to his fellow
and brings no harm against his neighbor;

4 the one who rejects the hateful idolator from
    his presence
but honors those who fear Yahweh;

the one who abandons his evil-doing
and does not return to it;

5 the one who does not take interest on a loan,
nor accept payment from those who are in need.

Anyone who lives like this
will not stumble ever.

Psalm 16 (15)

This is a song of confidence to be sung by those who have abjured the pagan worship of the Canaanites and placed their destiny in the hands of Yahweh, the God of Israel. The psalmist confesses that he used to be devoted to pagan deities (the "holy ones" and "princely ones"), but he has now abjured all forms of worship of them. Yahweh, he knows, has given him a better lot and will make all his future confident since he has power even over the nether-world. It has been much disputed by scholars whether this psalmist wrote in the hope of a life after death. The New Testament has understood verse 10 to refer to the resurrection of Jesus.

1   *A miktam of David.*

Watch over me, O God,
because I have entrusted myself to you.

2   I made this declaration:
"You, O Yahweh, are my sovereign, my happiness;
there is none higher than you."

3   As for those gods of the land
called "holy ones" and "princely ones"—
they used to be all my delight.

4   May their agonies be intense as labor pains,
and may their lustful desires go unfulfilled.

Never will my hands
pour out drink-offerings to them;
never will I drink to their names again.

5   Yahweh, you are the one who poured me the cup
of happiness,
you are the one who decided my lot.

6   The boundary lines mark off
a pleasant estate for me;
the Most High has determined my inheritance.

7   I praise Yahweh who counsels me;
     his heart instructs me
     during the watches of the night.

8   I keep my gaze fixed on Yahweh;
     never will I turn away from his right hand.

9   There is gladness in my heart
     and I feel boundless joy within me.
     My body too can rest unafraid

10   because you will not abandon me to Sheol;
     you will not consign to the Pit
     one who is devoted to you.

11   You will reveal the path of life to me.
     You will fill me with happiness in your presence,
     with delights forever at your right hand.

Psalm 17 (16)

A psalm of innocence. The psalmist prays this poem to pronounce that he is not devoted to idols but loyal to Yahweh. He may well be a public figure, possibly a king. Having pronounced that he is guiltless of false worship, he prays for the help of the Lord in overcoming his enemies, who are probably the enemies of the people, that is, of the faithful people.

1 *A prayer of David.*

Yahweh, hear my plea for justice;
listen to my ringing entreaty.
Turn your ear to my prayer.
Destroy lips that speak deceit.

2 Let the rightness of my case
shine out in your presence.
Let your eyes discern my innocence.

3 Search my heart, and even visit me by night!
Try me with fire,
but you will not find me worshipping images.

My mouth has not transgressed
4 by speaking to the work of human hands.
Rather, I have kept the words
that come from your lips.

5 My feet continue following the hard ways;
my steps have not strayed from your paths.

6 I call upon you!
If only you would answer me, O God.
Bend your ear down to me
and listen to what I say.

7 My Savior, cut down those who malign you![a]
With your right hand,
stop the mouths of those who assail you!

8 Protect me like your very eyes;
hide me in the shadow of your wings

9 from the ferocity of wicked men who lash out at
me,
from the enemies who hem me in.

10 They have no compassion in their hearts;
they speak with mouths full of pride.

11 Their feet are now surrounding me.
Their eyes are watching
to throw me into the land of the lost.

12 They are like the lion intent on its prey,
like a young lion crouching in ambush.

13 Rise up, O Yahweh;
confront their fury and overcome them.
Save my life from an evil death with your sword.

14 Slay them, O Yahweh, by your hand;
cut them off from among the living.
But satisfy the hunger of those you cherish.
May their children enjoy abundance,
and may they leave wealth for their offspring.

15 As for me,
at my justification I will look upon your face;
at my rising I will be satisfied by gazing on your
glory.[b]

---

a The translation of this verse is very uncertain. The present version follows
the interpretation of Fr. Dahood (PAB, I, p. 96).

b It is not clear here just what the psalmist had in mind. Some hold that he
spoke of the resurrection; but he may be referring to some legal or ritual
vindication.

Psalm 18 (17)

A royal hymn of thanksgiving. Though the title attributes the psalm to David himself, we cannot be sure of this nor can the occasion of the poem be assigned to any particular victory in history. The psalm was probably used by the king in Jerusalem, perhaps annually as a song of gratitude for all the deliverances that Yahweh had granted in the past. The first half of the psalm seems to be a hymn thanking the Lord for deliverance from death—not necessarily from physical death but from misfortunes which were the allies of death. The second half of the psalm speaks of rescue from more tangible enemies, perhaps the enemies who were the vassal kings and petty rulers of nations surrounding Judah.

1. *For the director: of the servant of Yahweh, David: he recited the lyrics of this song to Yahweh on the day Yahweh rescued him from the grip of all his enemies, especially from the grasp of Saul.*

2   And he said:
    I love you, Yahweh, my strength!

3   Yahweh is my rock and my fortress;
    My God is the one who rescues me.

    He is my mountain, and I trust in him.
    He is my shield, my mighty savior, my stronghold,
4   worthy of all praise.

Deliverance from Death

    I called Yahweh and he rescued me from my
        Enemy.
5   The swirls of death surrounded me;
    the currents of Belial were boiling up around me.

6   The cords of Sheol surrounded me;
    the traps of death came to meet me.

7   I was besieged but I called Yahweh;
    for help I cried to my God.

    My voice was heard in his palace;
    my call for help came to his ears.

8   At once the world below began to tremble and
        heave,
    and the foundations of the mountains shuddered:
    indeed they shook, for he was enraged.

9   Smoke billowed up from his nostrils;
    a consuming fire came from his mouth;
    glowing, flaming coals issued out from him.

10 He drew the heavens open and came down
    and a storm cloud was under his feet.

11 He mounted a cherub and flew,
    soaring on its outstretched wings.

12 He set darkness around him
    with the storm cloud as his pavillion.

13 From the splendor that surrounded him
    his dark clouds came swirling
    and hail and fiery lightning.

14 Yahweh thundered from the heavens;
    the Most High let his voice be heard.

15 He forged his arrows and shot them abroad.
    He multiplied his lightning-bolts
    and sent them flashing far and wide.

16 The sources of the sea could then be seen,
    and the foundations of the world were uncovered
    because you roared, O Yahweh,
    because you blew at them in your anger.

17 He reached down from on high and took me up;
    he drew me from the mighty waters.

18 He rescued me from my powerful Foe,
    though my Enemy was stronger than I.

19 He marched ahead of me on the day of my
        disaster;
    Yahweh was my staff of support.

20 He brought me out of death's broad domain,
    and he delivered me because he was delighted with
        me.

21 Yahweh repaid me because I was virtuous;
    he rewarded me because my hands were pure,

22 because I kept watch over my ways, O Yahweh,
    and did not sin, O my God.

23 His judgments are all before my eyes
    and I do not put aside his commands.

24 I am honest with him
    and I keep from offending him.

25 Yahweh repays me according to my innocence,
    because my hands are pure in his sight.

26 Toward the loyal man you are loyal yourself;
    toward the honest man you too are honest.

27 With the sincere man, you are sincere;
    but with the crafty man, you are devious yourself.

28 You, the Mighty One, deliver the lowly,
    but humiliate the eyes of the lofty.

29 You, O Yahweh, are my shining lamp.
    My God lights up my darkness.

Deliverance from Enemies

30 With you I can charge an army;
    with my God I can leap over defenses.

[34]

31 Complete is the dominion of God!
The word of Yahweh is sincere.
He is a sovereign who protects
all who flee to him for refuge.

32 What god is there other than Yahweh?
Who is a mountain except our God?

33 God is the one who girds me with strength:
he gives me complete dominion.

34 He makes my feet like the deer's
and causes me to stand on his heights.

35 He is the one who trained my hands for war
and lowered the magic bow[a] into my arms.

36 You gave me your shield of victory
and your right hand was my mainstay:
with your own triumph you made me great.

37 You made me run with giant steps;
my feet did not hesitate.

38 I pursued my foes and overtook them,
and I did not retreat
until I had made an end of them.

39 I dashed them down and they could not get up;
they fell at my feet.

40 You armed me with strength for war;
you made those who attacked me
fall prostrate beneath me.

41 You have made my enemies lower their necks
in submission under my feet.
I have exterminated my foes.

a The "magic bow", a phrase derived from Canaanite mythology, is a pictur-
esque image of the special divine help accorded the psalmist by the Lord.

[35]

42 They called out for help, but no savior was there.
They called: "Yahweh, Most High!"
but he did not answer them.

43 I pulverized them like dust on the wind;
I threw them out like street-sweepings.

44 You helped me escape the factions of the people
and made me the head of the nations.
A foreign people came to serve me:
45 as soon as they heard, they obeyed me.

Foreigners cringed before me;
46 foreigners surrendered to me,
and came out of their strongholds trembling.

Final Summation of Praise

47 Long live Yahweh!
And praised be my Mountain!
The God of my salvation be exalted!

48 He is the God who gave me victories
and made peoples subject to me.
He helped me escape from my Foe.

49 He placed me over my assailants;
he rescued me from those who slandered me.

50 God, Most High and Truthful, I will praise you
among the nations;
Yahweh, I will play music to your name.

51 You honor your king with victories;
you deal kindly with your anointed one,
with David and his descendants forever.

Psalm 19 (18)

Psalm 19 really consists of two poems, deliberately joined together. Verses 1-7, probably the older poem, glorify God's creation of the sun and the heavens. It may have a non-Israelite, Canannite origin. Verses 8-15 glorify the Lord's creation of the Law. These verses use the name "Yahweh" for God and are Israelite in their composition.

1   *For the director: a psalm of David.*

2   The heavens are proclaiming: Glory to God!
    The vault of the sky keeps telling:
    This is the work of his hands.

3   Each day relates it fully to the next;
    one night gives the knowledge to another.

4   There is no speaking, there are no words
    and not a sound is heard,

5   yet their call goes out through the whole world.

    Their story reaches the edge of the world,
    there he has placed a tent for the sun.

6   It comes out from there
    like a bridegroom from his bridal chamber;
    it rejoices like a champion running a race.

7   From the edge of the heavens it goes up;
    it crosses over to the farther side,
    without deviating from its course.

8   The instruction of Yahweh is complete,
    restoring my soul.

    The command of Yahweh is reliable,
    giving wisdom to my mind.

9   The precepts of Yahweh are right,
    gladdening my heart.

    The command of Yahweh is radiant,
    enlightening my eyes.

[37]

10 The authority of Yahweh is clear;
it stands firm forever.

The judgments of Yahweh are true;
every one of them is just.

11 They are more desirable than gold—
even the finest gold.

They are sweeter than honey—
even the sweetest honey.

12 Indeed, they enlighten your servant.
Keeping them wins an abundant reward.

13 Who knows his own mistakes?
Make me innocent of aberrations.

14 Restrain your servant from serving proud idols;
do not let them rule over me.

Then I shall be blameless;
innocent of the great rebellion.

15 May the words my mouth speaks delight you.
May the thoughts my heart ponders please you,
Yahweh, my Rock, my Redeemer.

Psalm 20 (19)

A liturgy for the king of Judah before he went into battle. Verses 1-6 comprise the public prayer for the king and his victory. Verses 7-10 are an answer from the Lord given by the priest or prophet at the temple. The psalm is filled with confident assurance that the Lord will help his anointed one overcome all his enemies.

1 *For the director: a psalm of David.*

2 May Yahweh give you victory in time of attack!
  May the name of Jacob's God be your defense!

3 May he send you help from the sanctuary;
  may he give you support from Zion!

4 May he remember all your offerings
  and regard as generous your burnt-sacrifices!

5 May he grant you your heart's desire
  and crown all your plans with success!

6 Then might we raise a shout in praise of your
      victory
  and wave our banners in the name of our God!
  May Yahweh grant all you ask!

7 Now I know that Yahweh is giving victory
  to the one he has anointed;
  he is answering him from his holy heaven
  and from his fortress his right hand is giving
      victory.

8 Some rely on chariots and some on horses as
      their strength,
  but we are mighty in the name of Yahweh,
      our God.

9 They will stagger and fall,
  but we will stand and be full of courage.

10 Yahweh has decided on victory for the king;
   he gave him triumph on the day we called.

Psalm 21 (20)

This psalm is related to Psalm 20 (19) in that the present psalm is a hymn of thanksgiving after a victory just as Psalm 20 was a prayer before battle. This poem reviews the king's requests for divine assistance and the Lord's response in the form of victory and prosperity and concludes with a verse of praise. In the Church this psalm has often been used as a hymn of praise for the resurrection of Christ, the King.

1 *For the director: a psalm of David.*

2 Your triumph, Yahweh, gives the king happiness.
  He is overjoyed because you brought him victory.

3 You gave him his heart's desire;
  you did not refuse his request.

4 You placed blessings of prosperity before him;
  you put a crown of fine gold on his head.

5 He asked you for eternal life[a]
  and you gave it to him—
  days without number, to eternity and beyond.

6 Great is his glory in your victory;
  you have endowed him with splendor and majesty.

7 You will surely give him blessings forever;
  with your presence, you will gladden him.

8 The king is putting his trust in Yahweh.
  He will not waver from his loyalty to the Most
      High.

9 Your left hand came down on all your enemies;
  your right, on all who hate you.

---

[a] The "eternal life" is not necessarily to be understood as life after death—it may well refer to the continuity of blessings on the king's descendants and nation.

10   At the time of your anger,
     you made them like a blazing oven, Yahweh.
     In your anger, you swallowed them
     and your fire devoured them.

11   You made their children vanish from the earth;
     they left no descendants among men.

12   They plotted to harm you and they schemed
         against you,
     but they could not prevail.

13   You made them lie prostrate
     when you aimed your arrows at their faces.

14   Rejoice in your triumph, Yahweh!
     In praise of your strength, we will sing hymns.

Psalm 22 (21)

This psalm begins in the style of a lament, but after verse 23 it has the characteristics of a hymn of praise. Some exegetes have thought that it may be two psalms joined, but it seems more probable that it is indeed one piece. Perhaps it is the song of a king who acted out annually his rescue from foreign enemies during the temple ritual. Whatever its origin, it was used by the evangelists to depict the suffering and death of Jesus, and Christians since that time have prayed this psalm to reflect on the Lord's passion and to join their sufferings to his.

1 *For the director: in the manner of "The Doe of the Dawn." A psalm of David.*

2 My God, my God, why have you forsaken me?
Why are you putting my cries for help
so far away from you?

3 My God, I cry out by day but there is no answer;
I call to you at night but there is no relief.

4 But you are the One enthroned in the Holy Place;
you are the Glory of Israel.

5 In you our fathers put all their trust;
they trusted and you rescued them.

6 To you they called for help and they were
delivered.
In you they trusted and they were not
disappointed.

7 But I am a worm, not a man,
the reproach of all men,
the one scorned by the nation!

8 All who see me laugh at me;
they mock and scoff and shake their heads:

9 "He lived for Yahweh—let Yahweh deliver him;
if Yahweh is pleased with him,
let him rescue him."

10 Yet it was you that took me from the womb
and caused me to be trustful at my mother's
breast.

11 To you I was given over from the time of my
birth;
since before I was born, my God has been you!

12 Do not go away from me now,
just when trouble is near,
just when there is no one to help.

13 A herd of bulls has surrounded me;
strong bulls of Bashan close in on me;

14 they open their jaws wide at me,
ravenous, roaring lions.

15 My strength drains away like water
and all my bones are out of joint.
My heart has turned to wax, melting inside me.

16 My throat is dry as burnt clay
and my tongue sticks to my mouth.
They have laid me in the mud of death.

17 Dogs have surrounded me;
a pack of evil-doers has encircled me.
They bite my hands and my feet,

18 so I can count each one of my bones.
They stare and gloat over me,

19 and distribute my garments among themselves
and cast lots for my clothes.

But you—
20 do not be far away from me, Yahweh!
You are my Help;
hurry to assist me!

21 Rescue my neck from the sword,
my face from the blade of the ax.

22 Save me from the jaws of the lion;
make me victorious over the horns of the wild
oxen.

23 Then I will be able to tell your name to my
brothers;
then I will be able to praise you in the
congregation:

24 "Praise Yahweh, all you that fear him;
give him glory, all you sons of Jacob;
stand in reverence for him, all you sons of Israel.

25 For he did not despise or abhor
the prayer of the afflicted man;
neither did he hide his face from him.
But when he called for help, he listened."

26 Many times over I repeat my praise
in the great assembly;
there I will keep my promises
in the presence of those who fear him.

27 The poor will eat and have their fill.
Those who seek Yahweh will praise him,
and their hearts will live for ever!

28 The ends of the earth will remember
and again turn to Yahweh.

All the tribes of the nations
will bow down before your face,

29 because Yahweh is truly the king,
the One ruling over the nations.

30 Even all those who sleep in the world below
will bow down to him,
and those who are going down into the Mud
will worship before him.
The Conqueror will restore their lives.

31   May my children serve him.
     May they speak of the Sovereign Lord forever.

32   May they come and tell of his justice;
     may they tell a people still to be born
     that he has taken action.

Psalm 23 (22)

Though this psalm is one of the most widely known pieces in all of biblical literature, its exact genre is far from certain. It seems to be a psalm of trust. The speaker may originally have been a king. He speaks of Yahweh as his shepherd who provides more than fully for all of his needs. He goes on to express his hope that he will be a guest in the house of Yahweh at a banquet. This might refer to participation in the liturgy, but it may also be an expression of longing for a more mystical union with the Lord.

1   *A psalm of David.*

    Yahweh is my shepherd:
    I will be in want of nothing.

2   He will have me lie down in green meadows;
    he will lead me to the waters, where there is rest,
3   and give new strength to my soul.

    He will direct me to lush pastures
    for the sake of his name.

4   Should I even walk in the darkness of death
    I would fear no evil,
    for you are beside me!
    Your rod, your staff—these will guide me!

5   You prepare a table for me
    in full view of my enemies.
    You anoint my head
    and fill my cup to overflowing.

6   Surely your goodness and your unfailing love will
        pursue me
    all the days of my life,
    and I will dwell in the house of Yahweh
    as long as days will last.

Psalm 24 (23)

This psalm is a processional hymn used at the autumnal feast. It celebrates the victory of the Lord over the forces of chaos, which was celebrated annually at the beginning of the new year. The song appears to have been used in connection with the ark of the covenant, which may have been carried in triumphal procession into the temple to the acclamations of the worshippers.

1 *A psalm of David.*

 To Yahweh belongs the earth and all it contains—
 the world and all who live in it.

2 He himself founded it upon the oceans,
 and established it upon the waters beneath.

3 Who may ascend Yahweh's mountain?
 who may stand in his holy shrine?

4 The man with clean hands and a pure heart,
 who does not lift his soul up to false gods
 and never swears by their deceit.

5 The blessing of Yahweh is his,
 and lavish bounty from the God who saves him.

6 Seek the God who is eternal;
 search for him who is present to Jacob.[a]

7 Lift your heads up in joy, you gates;
 rise up, doors of the Everlasting One,
 that the king of glory may come in!

8 Who is the king of glory?
 Yahweh, strong and mighty,
 Yahweh, valiant in combat.

---

[a] The translation of this verse is uncertain. The present version accepts the arrangement of the text of Fr. M. Dahood (PAB, I p. 152).

[47]

9 Lift your heads up in joy, you gates;
rise up, doors of the Everlasting One,
that the king of glory may come in!

10 Who is the king of glory?
The king of glory is Yahweh,
the Lord of power and might.

Psalm 25 (24)

This is an alphabetical acrostic, each new verse beginning with the next letter of the Hebrew alphabet. No date or life situation for its composition can be suggested with any certainty. Through most of the psalm the speaker seems to be an individual, and his poem is a lament. In the very last verse, however, the nation as a whole is prayed for, and perhaps the poem is a prayer for the people but this is far from certain.

1   *Of David.*

    I wait in suspense before you, O Yahweh.

2   My God, I trust in you.
    Do not let me be disgraced
    nor let my enemies gloat over me.

3   Surely those who call upon you
    will never feel ashamed:
    shamed rather are those who are false to you,
    who take no thought of you.

4   Show me your ways, Yahweh;
    teach your paths to me.

5   Make me walk in faithfulness to you, and teach
        me,
    because you are the God who saves me.
    You are the one I call upon all day long.

6   Remember your tenderness, Yahweh,
    and your constant love:
    they are from eternity.

7   Do not remember the sins of my youth,
    or my acts of rebellion.
    In your unfailing love remember me, Yahweh,
    for the sake of your goodness.

8   Yahweh, Most High and Truthful, is good and
        upright;
    he shows his way to sinners.

9 He guides the humble in knowing justice,
instructing them in his own ways.

10 All the ways of Yahweh are love and faithfulness
for those who keep the provisions of his covenant.

11 For the honor of your name, O Lord,
forgive my guilt—how great it is!

12 Who, then, is the man
who reveres Yahweh?
To him he will show the path to choose.

13 He will live in prosperity
and the Land will go to his children.

14 Intimacy with Yahweh is for those who revere
him,
and theirs to know his covenant.

15 My eyes are on Yahweh always:
He is the one who guides my feet away from the
snare.

16 Turn to me and treat me with mercy,
because I am all alone and treated wrongly.

17 Anguish oppresses my heart;
free me from all my distress.

18 Look at my misery and anxiety,
forgive me all my sins.

19 See my enemies—how they have multiplied!
They have a sinister hatred for me.

20 Guard me and rescue me.
I put my trust in you,
so do not let me be disappointed.

21 May Honesty and Integrity
be my attendants
while I make my appeal to you.

22 O God, ransom Israel from all her anxieties.

Psalm 26 (25)

A psalm of innocence. As in other such psalms, the poet repudiates all connection with idolatry and disloyalty to Yahweh. It is his longing to dwell in God's house, which seems to mean to enjoy some form of union with the Lord, seemingly more than just participation in external liturgy.

1 *Of David.*

Give judgment in my favor, Yahweh,
for I have walked with integrity.
I have trusted in Yahweh
and I have wavered not.

2 Prove me, O Yahweh, and try me;
test my heart and my mind,

3 for your unfailing love is before my eyes
and I have walked faithful to you.

4 I have not sat with men who worship idols
nor gone with those in darkness;

5 I have hated the company of evil men
and have not sat down with the wicked.

6 I have washed my hands with innocence
that I might join the procession around your altar,
Yahweh,

7 singing of your marvelous deeds
and recounting all your wonders.

8 Yahweh, I love to dwell in your house,
the shrine where your glory abides.

9 Do not sweep me away with sinners
nor cast me out with men who worship idols—

10 men whose left hand holds idols
and whose right hand is full of bribes.

11 As for me, I have walked with integrity;
redeem me and be merciful to me.

12 My feet have stood firmly among the upright;
in the assemblies I have adored Yahweh.

Psalm 27 (26)

Though many authors prefer to consider Psalm 27 as two distinct poems (verses 1-6 and verses 7-14), the reasons alleged for this division do not seem compelling. It seems better to regard the whole as a psalm of trust. The psalmist in his loyalty to the Lord longs to be with him. Though this may refer to a desire to be able to frequently celebrate the liturgy, it may be a request for spiritual union, perhaps even after death. The last eight verses of the psalm form a prayer for deliverance from enemies.

1 *Of David.*

Yahweh is my light and my salvation!
Whom shall I fear?

Yahweh is the fortress of my life!
Of whom shall I be afraid?

2 When evil men draw near me to swallow me up,
these enemies who assail me
are the very ones who stumble and fall.

3 If an army takes the field against me,
my heart will not be afraid.
If a line of battle advances on me,
I will keep on trusting even then.

4 One thing I have requested a hundred times, O
Yahweh;
this I seek:
to dwell in the house of Yahweh
all the days of my life;
to marvel at the beauty of Yahweh
and rise early every day at his palace.

5 In his dwelling he will protect me on the day of
evil.
He will conceal me deep inside his tent
and raise me up to his mountain.

6   So my head is already held high
    over the enemies who surround me.

    I will offer sacrifices in his tent,
    offering them with shouts of joy.
    I will sing and play music to Yahweh.

7   Hear my voice when I call, O Yahweh.
    Take pity on me and answer me.

8   My heart said: "Come and seek his face!"
    Your face, O Yahweh, I will seek:

9   do not hide your face from me.
    Do not turn your servant away in anger,
    but be the one who helps me.
    Do not forsake me—do not abandon me,
    God, my savior.

10 Even if my father and my mother abandon me,
    Yahweh will take me to himself.

11 Yahweh, point out your way;
    lead me on the path of uprightness
    because of my enemies.

12 Do not put me in the throat of my foes,
    because lying witnesses have come forward;
    they testify against me with malice.

13 I trust in the Conqueror
    that I will look upon the beauty of Yahweh
    in the land of the living.

14 Wait for Yahweh.
    Be strong and courageous of heart.
    And wait for Yahweh.

Psalm 28 (27)

Psalm 28 begins (verses 1-5) in the style of a personal lament but concludes with a joyous song of thanksgiving and a prayer for the king and the people. Perhaps it was originally a royal prayer. Whoever the psalmist was he prayed to be regarded as loyal to the worship of the Lord and further that idolaters reap the reward they had sown. Finally with praise and confidence he asked the Lord's blessing on his faithful people.

1 *Of David.*

> To you, Yahweh, I call;
> my Rock, do not be deaf to me!
> If you are silent,
> I will become like those who go down to the Pit.[a]

2 Hear my cry for mercy
> when I call to you for help,
> when I lift my hands toward your holy sanctuary.

3 Do not rank me with the wicked,
> nor with idolaters
> who speak words of peace to their neighbors
> while keeping malice in their hearts.

4 Repay them according to their works
> and the wickedness of their deeds.

> Requite them for what their hands have done!
5 Give them what they deserve.

> To the deeds of Yahweh,
> to the work of his hands they are blind.
> He will pull them down and never build them up!

6 Praise Yahweh, for he has heard
> my cry for mercy!

---

[a] A poetic name for the realm of the dead.

7 Yahweh is my Strength and my Shield;
my heart has trusted in him.

I have been renewed,
and my heart rejoices;
and with my song I will praise him!

8 Yahweh is a fortress for us and a refuge;
he is the deliverance of his Anointed.

9 Deliver your people and bless your heritage;
be their shepherd, and carry them forever.

Psalm 29 (28)

Psalm 29 is a hymn in praise of God probably used at the fall festival of the new year. This date formally inaugurated the season of the thunderstorms which bring the vital rains to Palestine. Hence, in this psalm, Yahweh is described as appearing in the power of a storm. Evidence is convincing that this psalm has borrowed generously from older Canaanite sources. It is possible that the storm was perhaps acted out symbolically in the temple where the psalm was used: the seven times repeated "voice of Yahweh," when spoken in Hebrew, has the effect of claps of thunder. The storm is described as passing from the sea (which stands for the original chaos) to the northern part of Israel and southern Lebanon. It is not unlikely that this psalm originated in the northern kingdom of Israel. The climax of the poem is the appearance of Yahweh in a theophany in the temple and blessing his people with peace and prosperity after the violence of the storm and the rains.

1   *A psalm of David.*

Give glory to Yahweh, you sons of God;
give Yahweh glory and praise.

2   Give glory to the name of Yahweh;
worship Yahweh, the Holy One, when he appears.

3   The voice of Yahweh—it echoes over the waters!
The God of glory thunders.
Yahweh is over the mighty waters;

4   The voice of Yahweh is power,
the voice of Yahweh is splendor.

5   The voice of Yahweh—it shatters the cedars!
Yahweh splinters the cedars of Lebanon.

6   He makes Lebanon leap like a calf,
Sirion[a] like a young wild ox.

---

a   A mountain in Lebanon, probably a Canaanite name for the better-known Mount Hermon.

7 The voice of Yahweh—it rends with shafts of fire!

8 The voice of Yahweh—it shakes the wilderness!
Yahweh shakes the wilderness of Kadesh![b]

9 The voice of Yahweh—it makes the doe give birth[c]
and strips the forest bare!

While a vision of the Glorious One
fills all the temple,
10 Yahweh sits enthroned since the chaos,
taking his seat as king forever.

11 Yahweh will give victory to his people;
Yahweh will bless his people with peace.

---

[b] This Kadesh is not the Kadesh in the wilderness of southern Palestine, but is
to be identified with a shrine in Syria, far to the north.
[c] The exact meaning of this obscure reference is unknown; perhaps it refers to
a now forgotten mythological symbolism.

Psalm 30 (29)

A song of personal thanksgiving. Though the circumstances of the use of this psalm are unknown, it seems to be a song of praise to Yahweh following the psalmist's recovery from some calamity, perhaps a serious illness. The title, which is, of course, a later addition, suggests that the song was used at the feast of the rededication of the temple, a feast which commemorated the "recovery" of the House of the Lord from the calamity of its defilement.

1 *A psalm; a song of the dedication of the House; of David.*

2 I will sing high praise about you, Yahweh,
because you have drawn me up.
You have not allowed my enemy to gloat over me.

3 O Yahweh, my God, I called upon you for help
and you healed me.

4 Yahweh, you have brought me up from Sheol;
you returned me to life
as I was going down into the Pit.

5 Make music for Yahweh, people devoted to him;
give praise to his holy name!

6 There is perdition in his anger,
but in his good pleasure, long life.

Weeping may lodge with you for the evening,
but in the morning come shouts of joy.

7 When I was prosperous and without cares,
I had said: "I will never stumble!

8 In your favor, Yahweh, you have made me
more firm than mighty mountains."
Then you hid your face and I was struck with
dismay.

9   O God, my Sovereign,
    I appeal to you for mercy.

10 "What gain would there be in my weeping,[a]
    in my going down to the land of decay?
    Will mud give you praise
    or proclaim your faithfulness?

11 O Yahweh, hear me and be merciful!
    Yahweh, be a helper to me!"

12 You turned my lament into joyful dancing.
    You undid my sackcloth
    and clothed me with gladness.

13 Now my heart can make music instead of
            mourning.
    O Yahweh, my God,
    I will thank you forever.

---

[a] This "weeping" is the mourning over death, in this case the psalmist's own.
He calculates that, since there is no possibility of liturgical praises for
Yahweh in the realm of the dead, it would be to Yahweh's advantage to
maintain him alive.

Psalm 31 (30)

This psalm begins as a long personal lamentation (verses 1-19) interspersed with protestations of loyalty to the Lord and innocence (verses 6-7; 15); finally in verses 20-25 the poem becomes a hymn of praise and thanksgiving for the poet's deliverance. The circumstances of the psalmist are uncertain. Perhaps he was in danger of death from sickness. Or perhaps it was the situation of a king under attack that inspired these lyrics. St. Luke's Gospel places the words of verse 6 into the mouth of Jesus as he was dying on the cross (Luke 23:46).

1 *For the director: a psalm of David.*

2 Yahweh, I have trusted in you.
Let me never be disgraced, Eternal One.

Deliver me because of your generosity.
3 Bend over me to hear me and hurry to rescue me.

4 Rock of refuge, be on my side.
Strong fortress, save me,
for you are my rock, my fortress.

You will guide me and lead me
for the honor of your name.

5 You will extricate me
from the web they have hidden for me,
because you are my refuge.

6 I entrust my spirit to your hands.
Redeem me, O Yahweh God.

7 In truth, I despise those who use helpless idols,
but I put my trust in Yahweh.

8 I will be glad and rejoice
because of your unfailing love.

When you saw my affliction,
you took care of my life against the Adversary.

9   You did not abandon me to the grasp of the
       Enemy
    nor make me walk in the wide expanse of Sheol.

10   Have mercy on me, Yahweh, for I am in
       adversity;
    my eyes are dimmed from grief;
    my throat and my vitals are ravaged.

11   My life is worn away with sorrow
    and my years with sighing.
    My strength is wavering under misery,
    my bones are weak (12) and my heart is spent.

    I have become an object of reproach
    even to my neighbors,
    a disaster and an object of dread to my friends.

13   I have withered up like a dead man without heart
    and become like a broken jar.

14   For I hear many whisper, "Terror on every side."[a]
    When they conspire against me,
    they plot to take my life.

15   But as for me, I put my trust in you, O Yahweh,
    and I declare: "You are my God."

16   Every stage of my life is in your hands.
    Rescue me from the grip of my enemies
    and from those who persecute me;

17   turn your face toward your servant with favor.
    Save me in your unfailing love.

---

[a] "Terror on every side": an expression found some half dozen times in Jeremiah, who used it so often as a warning of Yahweh's intended punishment for Jersualem that the crowds made it into a scornful nickname for the prophet. Perhaps the psalmist is being mocked in the same fashion.

18 Yahweh, do not let me be disgraced,
because I call to you.

Let disgrace fall upon the wicked
and let them be thrown into Sheol.

19 Let lying lips be muzzled—
those that speak in insolence and pride and
      arrogance
against the virtuous man.

20 How great is the goodness
which you have stored up
for those who reverence you.
You have kept it for those who confide in you
where the sons of men may see it.

21 You hide them under the screen of your presence
far from the intrigues of men.
You keep them inside your tent,
safely away from wrangling tongues.

22 Praise to Yahweh
because he showed me the wonder of his kindness
from the city of his fortress!

23 In alarm I had said, "I am shut out of your
      sight."
But you heard my pitiful cry when I called to you
      for help.

24 Love Yahweh, all you his loyal servants!
Yahweh protects the faithful
but will pay the arrogant in full.

25 Be strong and let your hearts be bold,
all of you whose hope is in Yahweh!

Psalm 32 (31)

The second penitential psalm. This seems to be a song of thanksgiving for a man released from some suffering, perhaps sickness, which was the result of sin. In recounting his forgiveness and deliverance the psalmist speaks in the manner of an Israelite wisdom teacher.

1   *Of David. A maskil.*

    How happy the man whose rebellion is forgiven,
    his sin covered over!

2   How happy the man Yahweh does not accuse of
       malice,
    who has no deceit in his spirit!

3   But I was drying up ᵃ and my bones were wasting
       away;
    I groaned all the day.

4   By day and by night
    your hand, O Most High, was heavy.
    Mighty God, I was overcome as by the summer
       drought.

5   I confessed my sin to you—
    I did not conceal my guilt.

    I said: "O Most High, O Yahweh,
    I will acknowledge my acts of rebellion."
    And you removed my guilt and my sin.

6   Let every devoted man, therefore, pray to you.
    If an army draws near, or flood waters crest,
    they will not reach him.

ᵃ This version follows Dahood's suggestion: (PAB, I, p. 194). The present Hebrew text reads: "When I was silent, my bones wasted away." The present version seems more consistent with the imagery of this psalm.

7 You are a place where I can hide.
Guard me, my Refuge, from the one who attacks
      me;
deliver me and surround me.

8 "I shall instruct you
and show you the way you must walk by.
My eyes will not be closed upon you.

9 Do not become like a stallion or mule:
they have no sense—

their boisterousness must be bridled
with muzzle and halter.
Only then can you approach them."

10 How often the wicked man must grieve!
But the one who trusts in Yahweh
is surrounded with his unfailing love.

11 Be glad in Yahweh, you just men,
and leap for joy.
Sing out, all of you that have upright hearts.

Psalm 33 (32)

A hymn that extols the Lord as Creator of all things and expresses confidence in Yahweh's strength and all-guiding providence. This hymn may well be very ancient. It was probably used at the new year festival in the autumn when the wonders of creation were celebrated and the covenant with the Lord was renewed; hence the permanence of the creation and of the works of the Lord is mentioned, and God's care for his people and his victory over the nations and the forces of death are also recalled.

1 All of you who are upright, sing for joy to
       Yahweh!
  Give praise to the Glorious One,
  all of you who are upright.

2 Praise Yahweh with a harp;
  on a lute of ten strings play to him!

3 Sing him a new song!
  Make beautiful music with gladness!

4 The word of Yahweh is true;
  the works of his hands are worthy of trust.

5 He loves what is just and what is right.
  The earth is full of Yahweh's unfailing love.

6 At the word of Yahweh the heavens were made;
  a breath of his created all the lights that are
      in them.

7 He confined the waters of the sea in a vessel;
  he put the primeval abyss in his storehouses.

8 Give reverence to Yahweh, all the earth;
  all peoples of the world, stand in awe of him.

9 For he is the one who spoke,
  and everything came to be;
  he is the one who gave the command,
  and there stood everything.

10 Yahweh breaks up the plan of the nations;
   he frustrates the schemes of the peoples.

11 The plan of Yahweh will stand forever;
   the designs of his heart will last age after age.

12 Happy the nation that Yahweh, its God, has
          blessed!
   Happy the people he has chosen to be his own!

13 Yahweh looks from heaven
   and sees all the sons of men;

14 from the throne where he presides
   he looks upon everyone who dwells on his earth.

15 The Creator gazes on their hearts;
   he discerns everything they do.

16 No king wins the victory by the size of his forces,
   no warrior wins deliverance
   by the greatness of his strength.

17 The horse cannot be relied on for safety;
   even with all his power he does not escape.

18 But see how Yahweh watches over those who
          reverence him
   and over those who hope for his unfailing love.

19 He will deliver their souls from death;
   from that Ravenous One he will rescue their lives.

20 We are waiting in hope for Yahweh;
   he is our warrior and our shield.

21 Our hearts rejoice in him;
   we trust in his holy name.

22 Let your unfailing love come upon us, Yahweh,
   just as we have put our hope in you.

Psalm 34 (33)

A song of thanksgiving for an individual. Though the origin of the psalm cannot be known for certain, it has been plausibly suggested that it was a votive tablet, an inscribed record of help received from Yahweh and then deposited as a memorial in a shrine. In some verses the psalmist speaks in the fashion of a wisdom teacher and perhaps is using his experiences to teach others. The logical progression of the poem is not exact because it is an alphabetical poem and hence one verse does not follow after the other in an exact thought sequence.

1 *Of David: when he feigned insanity in the presence of Abimelech who expelled him and he left.*

2 I will bless Yahweh at all times;
   his praise will continuously be in my mouth.

3 My soul will glory in Yahweh.
   May the lowly hear of it and be glad!

4 O glorify Yahweh with me!
   Let us exalt his name together!

5 I sought Yahweh and he answered me
   and he delivered me from all my anxieties.

6 Men look to him and their faces glow with joy;
   never will they be ashamed.

7 This poor man called out and Yahweh was
         listening;
   from all his troubles he saved him.

8 Yahweh's angel is encamped around those
         who reverence him,
   and he rescues them.

9 Taste and eat your fill!
   How good Yahweh is!
   How happy the man who takes shelter in him!

10 Live in reverence for him,
    you holy people of Yahweh;
    those who fear him have need of no other thing.

11 The wealthy will be in want and hunger,
    but those who seek Yahweh will never lack
        any blessing.

12 Approach, my sons, and listen to me;
    I will teach you to reverence Yahweh.

13 Which of you desires life
    and longs to live happily?

14 Guard your tongue from evil,
    and your lips from speaking deceit.

15 Turn away from evil and do good;
    search for peace and pursue it.

16 Yahweh watches over just men;
    when they call for help, he listens to them.

17 Yahweh's fury opposes men who do evil;
    he will efface their memorials from the land.

18 The just call out for help and Yahweh is listening,
    and from all their tribulations he rescues them.

19 Yahweh is close to those whose hearts are broken;
    he delivers those who are bruised in spirit.

20 Many are the sorrows of a just man,
    but Yahweh rescues him from them all.

21 He guards every one of his bones;
    not one will be broken.

22 Evil will kill the wicked man
    and those who hate the just man will be chastised.

23 Yahweh will ransom the lives of those who serve
        him
    and all who take refuge in him will not perish.

Psalm 35 (34)

This psalm seems to be a personal lament, but it probably was originally the anguished prayer of a king. It may have been used during the annual celebration of the re-enthronement of the king when, just before his reign was celebrated, he prayed for the defense of the Lord against his enemies, against whom he would otherwise be helpless.

1   *Of David.*

     Contend, Yahweh, with those who contend against
        me;
     fight with those who are fighting me.

2   Grasp your shield and armor;
     rise up to help me.

3   Raise your javelin and spear
     to confront those who pursue me.
     Say to me, "I am your victory!"

4   Shame and dishonor on those who seek my life!
     Let those who scheme to hurt me
     be turned back in confusion.

5   Like chaff before the wind, let them be driven
     with the angel of Yahweh behind them!

6   Darkness and destruction be their end,
     pursued by the angel of Yahweh!

7   Stealthily they set a trap for me with their net;
     stealthily they dug a pit for me.

8   Let ruin come upon him by surprise.
     Let him be caught in his own net;
     let him fall into his own pit.

9   Then I will be overjoyed in Yahweh;
     I will rejoice at his victory.

10   All my bones will exclaim,
     "Yahweh, who can compare with you?

     You save the weak man
     from one who is too strong for him,
     and the man who is poor and needy
     from the one who is despoiling him."

11   Witnesses for an idol which I do not acknowledge
     are taking the stand;
     they are putting me to an ordeal. [a]

12   They repay my kindness with evil.
     They despoil my soul. [b]

13   When they were suffering,
     I was wearing sackcloth;
     I afflicted myself with fasting.

     My prayer was resting on my breast
14   like a friend or brother.
     I walked about like one in mourning for his
           mother,
     bent down, and dressed in black.

15   But if I limped or stumbled
     they gathered around rejoicing;
     they flocked together to strike me
     but I paid no heed.
     They did not stop taunting me.

16   They surrounded me to mock me
     and ground their teeth at me.

17   How much longer, O Sovereign, will you look on?
     Rescue my neck from their ravages;
     save my face from these lions.

---

a The enemies of the psalmist accuse him of turning away from the Lord and
   having recourse to idolatry, which he denies.
b A possible translation. The Hebrew is unclear.

18   I will thank you in the great assembly;
amid the great throng I will praise you.

19   Do not let my treacherous enemies gloat over me;
do not let those who hate me
slyly wink at each other.

20   They are surely not whispering "Peace!" to each
other;
they are making attacks
and hatching plots against the oppressed of the
land.

21   They open their mouths wide at me,
saying, "At last we see it with our own eyes!"

22   Observe, Yahweh!
Do not be silent!
Do not be far from me, my Sovereign!

23   Awake, rise up, come to my defense;
my God and my Sovereign, come to contend for
me!

24   Defend me, Yahweh, my God—
your justice demands it.
Do not let them gloat over me.

25   Do not let them say in their hearts:
"How satisfying it is,"
nor let them declare:
"We swallowed him in one bite!"

26   Dishonor and shame on all
who rejoice at my mortal terror!
Let disgrace and shame cover all who make boasts
over me!

27 Let those who are pleased at my vindication
   cry out for joy and be glad.
   Forever let them say:
   "Great is Yahweh,
   who takes pleasure in the prosperity of his
      servant!"

28 Then your justice will be on my tongue.
   I will speak your praises all the day long.

Psalm 36 (35)

This psalm seems to be a didactic poem which concludes with a prayer. The burden of the psalm is the contrast between the man who has a false faith, that is, a trust in idols, and those who are loyal to the covenant with the Lord. The wicked idolater becomes rigid in his stand for evil, while the care of Yahweh for those faithful to him knows no bounds and is graphically described as the source of mystic blessings. Perhaps there is even a suggestion in verses 9 and 10 that one of those blessings is a life beyond the grave, though certainty about this matter is not possible here. Verses 11-13 are a prayer for those who abide by the covenant, among whom the poet wishes to count himself. The last lines of the psalm return to the opening theme: the idol worshippers will fall into Sheol.

1   *For the director: of the servant of Yahweh, of David.*

2   This is the intention of the rebellious man:
    "In my heart I have decided to do evil!"
    There is no fear of God in him at all.

3   What he calls "god" makes it easy
    for him to speak evil.

4   The words he speaks are of idolatry and deceit.
    He lacks the sense to act wisely or well;

5   he lies awake to plot acts of idolatry.
    He has taken his stand on a path that is evil
    and he never regrets his decision.

6   Yahweh, your unfailing love comes from the
            heavens,
    and your faithfulness is as high as the clouds.

7   Your generosity is like the mountains of God
    and your care vast as the great abyss.
    To man and beast you give abundance.

8   How precious, Yahweh, is your unfailing love!
    Gods and the sons of men find refuge
    in the shadow of your wings.

9   They are filled up with the richness of your house.
You give them drink
from the river of your abundance.

10   For with you is the source of life
and in your lands we see light.

11   Continue your unfailing love for those who
acknowledge you as God,
and your generosity toward men of upright heart.

12   Let the foot of pride not overtake me
nor the hand of evil throw me down!

13   See how the worshippers of idols have fallen.
They are thrown down and they will be unable to
rise.

Psalm 37 (36)

This is an alphabetical poem, each new section beginning with
the next letter of the Hebrew alphabet. It is a psalm of wisdom.
The speaker is (or assumes the role of) an elderly man who
seeks to inculcate a calm trust in the providence of God into
his young pupils who tend to be impatient with the visible
prosperity of the wicked. In this psalm these are apparently
men who are faithless to Yahweh and ready partakers in the
cults of idols. The allusions to fertility and withering in verses
19 and 20 suggest that the wicked are men who participate in
Canaanite fertility cults. The psalmist assures his students that
the prosperity of these faithless men, who cannot abide the just
men in their midst, is illusory and that ultimately Yahweh's
care for his devoted ones will vindicate their fidelity.

1 *Of David.*

   Do not be troubled because of people who are
         malicious;
   do not be envious of those who do evil.

2 They will soon wither like the grass
   and fade like the green of the fields.

3 Trust in Yahweh and do good
   so you will dwell in the land
   and have your food from its fruitfulness.

4 Find your delight in Yahweh
   and he will give you the desires of your heart.

5 Commit your destiny to Yahweh;
   trust in him and he will help you.

6 He will make your virtue shine as bright as the
         sun
   and the justice of your cause like the noonday
         brilliance.

7 Wait quietly for Yahweh, and keep hoping in him;
do not be agitated about the man who forges his
own prosperity
nor about one who brings his wicked schemes to
success.

8 Refrain from fury and forsake passion.
Do not be vexed because that begets only harm.

9 Those who are bent on evil will be cut down,[a]
but those who call upon Yahweh will inherit the
land.

10 After a little while, the wicked will have no more
power:
examine their shrine and you will find it deserted.

11 But the meek will possess the land
and delight in the fullness of prosperity.

12 The wicked hatch plots against the virtuous man
and gnash their teeth at the sight of him.

13 The Sovereign will laugh at them
because he knows when his day is coming.

14 The wicked draw their swords and bend their
bows;
they intend to bring down the poor and the
needy
and to slaughter men whose lives are upright.

15 Their swords will pierce their own hearts
and their bows will be splintered into pieces.

16 The little which the virtuous have
is better than the wealth of the wicked,

a It is evident that those who are "bent on evil" are the opposites of those who
"call upon Yahweh," that is, malicious idolaters.

[77]

17 because the strong arm of the wicked will be
        broken
    while Yahweh will continue to support the
        virtuous.

18 Yahweh provides for the days of honest men
    and their heritage will last forever:

19 they will not dry up in times of drought
    and in days of famine they will have an
        abundance.

20 The wicked will wither,
    and all the enemies of Yahweh will vanish
    like the draws which dry up.
    More quickly than smoke they will vanish.

21 The wicked borrow and do not repay,
    but the virtuous are open-handed and give freely;

22 those he has blessed will possess the land,
    but those he has cursed will be destroyed.

23 The steps of a man are made steady by Yahweh
    who makes his way secure.

24 If he starts to fall he will not be thrown down
    because Yahweh keeps holding him by the hand.

25 I was once young and now I am old,
    and I have never seen a virtuous man forsaken
    or his children begging their bread.

26 He is always lending and giving generously
    and his children are destined for blessings.

27 Turn away from evil and do good
    and you will abide forever,

28 because Yahweh loves the just man
    and will not forsake those loyal to him.

    They will be preserved forever
    but the children of the wicked will be
        exterminated.

29 The virtuous will inherit the land
    and they will reside on it forever.

30 The mouth of the virtuous man murmurs wise
        words
    while his speech is ever just.

31 The law of his God is in his heart,
    and so his steps will never falter.

32 The wicked man watches for the one who is
        virtuous
    and seeks an occasion to take his life;

33 but Yahweh will not abandon him
    or let him be condemned when he is brought to
        trial.

34 Wait for Yahweh and keep to his way
    and he will raise you up to inherit the land.
    When the wicked are cut down,
    you will see it.

35 I have seen a wicked man standing starkly,
    towering like a tree thriving in its native soil.

36 But he passed away and was no more;
    though I searched for him, he was not to be
        found.

37 Just watch the man of integrity,
    just observe the man of honesty;
    there is a future for the man of peace.

38 But rebels will be destroyed one and all;
    the future of the wicked will be cut off.

39 But vindication for the virtuous man comes
     from Yahweh.
  He is their stronghold in times of distress.

40 Yahweh will help them
  and he will rescue them;
  he will save them from the malicious
  because they take shelter with him.

Psalm 38 (37)

The third penitential psalm. This poem is the prayer of a sick man. But its measured cadences and well-chosen phrases, selected from the best examples of Israelite lamentations, were probably not composed in the midst of a wasting disease. It was doubtless used as a ritual prayer for the sick and perhaps even on the occasion of other calamities. In verses 2-12 the psalmist describes the misery of his illness. He is set upon by idolaters to have recourse to false gods (verse 13), but he puts all his faith in the Lord who will (he is certain) come to his rescue (verses 14-23).

1   *A psalm of David. For a memorial.*

2   Yahweh, do not convict me when you are angry,
    or punish me in your rage.

3   For your arrows have gone through me
    and your hand has come down upon me.

4   There is no soundness in my flesh
    because of your anger;
    there is no peace in my bones because of my sin.

5   My iniquities have fallen on my head—
    a burden far too heavy for me to bear.

6   My sores are festering and running
    because of my foolishness.

7   I am bent over, bowed very deeply;
    all day long I walk in mourning.

8   I am racked with searing pain within me,
    and there is no soundness in my body.

9   I am weak and completely broken;
    I moan in the anguish of my heart.

10 Lord, all my longing lies open to you
    and all my sighing is never far from you.

11 My heart is pounding, my strength has failed me;
the light of my eyes, even that is gone.

12 My dear ones and my friends stay away from my
plague;
my family, too, stands far away from me.

13 Those who are seeking my life are laying snares
for me,
and those who wish me evil cast harmful spells
and mutter about lying idols all day long.

14 But I am like a deaf man and I will not listen,
like a mute who does not open his mouth.

15 I am like a man
who does not answer because he will not hear.

16 It is you, Yahweh, that I am waiting for!
It is you that will answer, O God, my Sovereign,

17 when I pray:
"Do not allow them to gloat over me,
and if my foot slips, do not let them rejoice!"

18 My sin is always standing there
and my pain is with me continually.

19 I keep repeating my evil to myself,
anxious because of my sin.

20 The enemies of my life are mighty,
and those who treacherously hate me are many.

21 Those who return evil for blessing
accuse me when I search for good.

22 Do not abandon me, Yahweh;
my God, do not go far away from me.

23 Come quickly to my help, my Sovereign,
to my salvation.

Psalm 39 (38)

A reverie on the brevity and vanity of human life. Somewhat in the style of the author of Ecclesiastes, the psalmist recounts the tale of how he struggled with the meaning of life. He begins by recalling the resolution that he had taken not to think too deeply about this enigma, but he proceeds to tell how his thoughts caused him more agitation than he could contain. Somewhat in the style of Job, he prays that God will give him some respite from suffering in this life so that he may have a small period of happiness before he goes off to the grave. His anxiousness about all of this was made poignant by the knowledge that the evil man without faith seemed to enjoy prosperity nonetheless (verse 2).

1 *For the director: of Jeduthun. A psalm of David.*

2 This was the resolution I had taken:
"I will watch my ways lest I sin with my tongue;
I will keep a muzzle over my mouth
even though the wicked man gloats in my
    presence."

3 I bound myself to silence;
I refrained from speaking, but my anguish only
    increased.

4 My heart was burning within my breast,
and while I pondered, a fire blazed up.
I began to speak:

5 "Let me know, Yahweh, my final destiny.
Just how many days will I have?
Let me know how short my life will be."

6 Behold, mere handbreaths you have made my
    days;
and my lifespan—it is as nothing in your sight.

Alas! All is vapor!
Every man is a figment.

7   Indeed, it is all but a shadow—a man living his
        life;
    his feverish activity—it is just a vapor;
    he amasses a fortune—yet he knows not who will
        collect it.

8   But now what am I hoping for, my Sovereign?
    My expectations? You are all I have.

9   Deliver me from all my acts of rebellion.
    Do not make of me a fool's reproach.

10 I was muzzled and did not open my mouth.
    If only you would act . . .

11 Remove your scourge from me
    because I am weak from the blows of your hand.

12 You correct a man for his guilt by striking him.
    Like a moth you nibble away his life.
    Alas, a vapor is every man!

13 Hear my prayer, Yahweh!
    O God, listen to my call!
    Do not be deaf to my tears!
    All I am is an outsider with you,
    a foreigner, like all my fathers.

14 Turn your eyes away from me;
    let me be cheerful
    before I go away and there be no more of me.

Psalm 40 (39)

Because verses 14-18 of this psalm are substantially the same as Psalm 70, many scholars have thought that Psalm 40 is a composite poem made up of a hymn of thanksgiving and followed by an urgent lament. But it seems better to consider this psalm as a unified composition. It may have been a poem for the royal ritual at the annual enthronement feast. The king proclaims that Yahweh has delivered him from the dangers posed by his enemies (verses 2-6); he relates that Yahweh has elevated him not because of sacrifices offered, but because he has kept Yahweh's law and proclaimed his will to all the people (verses 7-12); finally he prays his requests for rescue and prosperity for the future (verses 13-18). The Epistle to the Hebrews (10:5ff) quotes this psalm to explain how Jesus brought about the redemption of mankind.

1   *For the director: a psalm of David.*

2   I called and called on Yahweh:
    he bent down to me and listened to my cry for
        help.

3   He lifted me out of the Pit of Destruction,
    out of the muck and the mire;
    he set my feet upon rock and gave me a firm
        footing.

4   He put a new song in my mouth—
    a hymn of praise to our God.
    Many see and are filled with awe
    and put their trust in Yahweh.

5   Happy the man who makes Yahweh his hope
    and does not turn to idols or to fraudulent images!

6   You have done many things, O Yahweh.
    In your wonders and your designs for us
    you have no equal.
    I would relate them and speak of them,
    but they surpass all telling.

7 You had no interest in sacrifice or offering,
but you made my ears attentive.
Burnt-offering and sin-offering you did not
    require.

8 Then I said: "See, I am coming."
In the scroll it is written for me:

9 "I was to delight
in doing your good pleasure, my God,
and your law was to be deep in my heart."

10 In the great assembly
I proclaimed the good news of your generosity.
And I did not close my lips—
Yahweh, you know that.

11 I have not kept your generosity hidden within
    my heart
but have told about your faithfulness and your
    victory.

I did not conceal from the great assembly
your unfailing love and faithfulness.

12 O Yahweh, you did not cut me off from your
    tenderness;
your unfailing love and your faithfulness
were my constant attendants.

13 Evils have crowded in on me
until there is no numbering them.

My wicked acts have caught up with me
and I cannot escape.
There are more of them than hair on my head
and my heart has deserted me.

14 Hurry, Yahweh, and rescue me!
Come quickly, Yahweh, and help me!

15 Let those who seek my life to shear it off
be humiliated and disgraced.

16 Let those who would enjoy my misfortunes
shrink back in shame.
May those who jeer at me
be astonished at their own defeat.

17 May all who seek you
rejoice and be glad because of you.
Let those who love your deliverance
always say: "Great is Yahweh!"

18 I am afflicted and poor but my Sovereign will
think of me.
My Help and my Rescue are you, my God;
do not delay!

Psalm 41 (40)

The prayer of a man who is sick. This psalm begins with a blessing for the man who has "wisely ruled his speech", that is, he has kept his tongue from invoking idols. In verses 6-10 the psalmist recounts the activities of his enemies: they try to cast spells on him and are quite overeager to pronounce him incurable. Verses 11-13 are the psalmist's request to Yahweh for his deliverance. Verse 14 does not belong to the psalm but is a later addition, a doxology to indicate that this point is the end of what in Jewish tradition was Book I of the psalter.

1 *For the director: a psalm of David.*

2 How happy the man who wisely rules his speech!
   On the day of death Yahweh will rescue him.

3 May Yahweh protect him, and give him life.
   May he bless him on the earth
   and not place him in the throat of his Enemy.

4 May Yahweh care for him as he lies languishing.
   May he lift him up from his bed and vanquish his
      sickness.

5 I said: "Have pity on me, Yahweh,
   heal me, even though I have sinned against you."

6 My foes are discussing my death:
   "When will he die? When will his name perish?"

7 And if one comes to visit, his heart speaks of
      calamity;
   he gathers up the bad reports
   and gossips when he goes out of the door.

8 They whisper together against me;
   all my enemies, O Most High, scheme the worst
      about me:

9 "A deadly spell has been cast on him—
   he is lying in his bed and will never get up again."

[88]

10 Even the friend I trusted, the one who ate my
        bread,
    he has lifted his heel against me.

11 But, Yahweh, have pity on me and help me arise
    so I may pay them back.

12 I will know you are pleased with me
    if my foe does not shout in triumph over me.

13 I have kept my integrity.
    Hold on to me and stand me forever in your
        presence.

                    *   *   *

14 Praise Yahweh, the God of Israel,
    from eternity to eternity.

Psalm 42 (41)

Psalms 42 and 43 probably are a single psalm although in all versions and in the Hebrew itself they are classed as two psalms. This psalm seems to be a prayer of an individual in the form of a lament. Why the psalmist sings this very moving and sad song is unclear: he seems to feel himself far from the presence of God. Some scholars feel that this distance is a physical one: he is far removed from the temple and its worship. Verse 3 seems at first sight to support this theory. Yet there is much else in the psalm that seems to suggest that it is just in his inner self that the psalmist feels far removed from God. He seems to himself to be in the realm of the dead (verses 7-8) which is as far from God as one can imagine oneself. Through it all he maintains a hopeful confidence that he will soon be with the Divine Presence again.

1   *For the director: a maskil; of the sons of Korah.*

2   Just as a deer sighs for the running streams,
    my soul sighs, O God, for you.

3   With all my soul I thirst for God—
    I thirst for the living God.
    When will I come and imbibe the Presence of
        God?

4   My tears have been my food day and night,
    while all the day long I am asked:
    "Where is your God?"

5   When I remember these things
    my soul is distressed:
    how I crossed the Enclosure;

    I bowed down toward the House of God
    while cries of joy and thanksgiving rang out
    as a noisy crowd celebrated a feast.

6   Why are you depressed, my soul,
    and why do you sigh within me?
    Wait for God—I will praise him again,
    my Salvation, my divine Presence, (7) my God.

    My soul is depressed
    so I remember you from the land of ravines and
        pitfalls,[a]
    from the mountains at the edge of the nether-
        world.

8   Where one abyss and then another re-echoes
    with the sound of your thunder,
    all your breakers and waves pass over me.

9   By day Yahweh sends his unfailing love
    and by night I sing a hymn,
    a prayer to the God of my life.

10   I say to God, my Rock:
    "Why have you forgotten me?
    Why do I walk in gloom
    while the Enemy torments me
11   and Death is in my bones?"

    All the day long
    my adversaries say to me with disdain:
    "Where is your God?"

12   Why are you depressed, my soul,
    and why do you sigh within me?
    Wait for God—I will praise him again,
    my Salvation, my divine Presence, my God.

a The fearsome landscape here described constitutes some main features of Sheol.

Psalm 43 (42)

This psalm is doubtless a continuation of Psalm 42. While the previous poem concentrated on describing the state of the poet, this conclusion of the prayer turns wholly to God with the psalmist's request: that he may come back to the presence of God.

1 Judge me, O God, and plead my case.
  Help me escape from a godless nation
  and from the deceitful and crooked man.

2 For you are my stronghold, O God:
  Why do you thrust me away from you?
  Why do I walk in gloom
  while the Enemy torments me?

3 Send your light and your truth;
  let them lead me
  and bring me to your holy mountain,
  to your dwelling.

4 Let me come to the altar of God,
  to God, the joy of my young life;
  let me praise you on the lyre, O God, my God.

5 Why are you depressed, my soul,
  and why do you sigh within me?
  Wait for God—I will praise him again,
  my Salvation, my divine Presence, my God.

Psalm 44 (43)

A national lament. This psalm seems to be a song of the northern kingdom of Israel, composed during a time of great calamity. The psalmist reviews the favor God showed to his people in former times (verses 2-9); then he contrasts the previous prosperity with the present state of abject defeat (verses 10-18). Verses 19-23 are a protestation of continued loyalty to God and his covenant. The psalm concludes with a desperate call for the immediate assistance of God (verses 24-27).

1   *For the director: a maskil of the sons of Korah.*

2   O God, we used to listen to the tales our fathers
       told!
  What wonders you worked in their days!
  What your hands did in times long gone!

3   You dispossessed nations
  and planted your people instead.
  Other peoples you smashed,
  your own you made take root.

4   It was not by their sword
  that they gained possession of the land
  nor was it by their own arm
  that they won the victory.

  Rather, it was by your right hand,
  and by your arm and the light from your face,
  because they were your delight.

5   You are my king, my God, my law-giver,
  the salvation of Jacob.

6   Through you we rammed our adversaries;
  in your name we trampled our assailants.

7   I did not put my trust in my bow—
  my sword did not make me the victor:

8 you it was who helped us conquer our enemies,
   and those who hated us you put to shame.

9 In God we used to boast all day long;
   and we would have praised your name forever.

10 But now you have thrust us away from you
       and disgraced us,
   you will not march with our armies;

11 you make us retreat from our enemy,
   and those who hate us have despoiled us.

12 You made us like a flock ready to be devoured
   and scattered us among the nations.

13 You have sold your people for a trifle
   and you made no profit on the sale.

14 You have exposed us to the barbs of our
       neighbors,
   an object of mockery and derision for all those
       around us.

15 You have made us the joke of the nations;
   they shake their heads at us
   as if we were of no account.

16 All the day long my disgrace confronts me,
   and in shame I hide my face

17 from the cries of those who mock me and insult
       me,
   from my enemies who are seeking vengeance.

18 Every indignity has come upon us,
   even though we have not forgotten you,
   even though we have not been disloyal
   to the covenant you made with us.

19 Our hearts have not crept away from you
   nor have our feet stepped from your path.

20 Yet you have crushed us where the primeval
      monsters are
and covered us with total darkness.[a]

21 If we had forgotten the name of our God,
or raised our palms toward a foreign god,

22 would God not have probed this outrage,
since he knows the secrets of the heart?

23 But on your account we are slain all the day long:
we are listed as sheep to be slaughtered.

24 Awake! Lord, why are you sleeping?
Arise! Do not thrust us away from you forever!

25 Why do you turn your face away?
Why do you forget our suffering and our misery?

26 We are up to our necks in the mud;
our bodies are prone in the world below.[b]

27 Arise and help us!
Redeem us for the sake of your unfailing love.

---

a The present condition of the people resembles a stay in the chaos of old
before Yahweh had made the world fit for people to live in.
b The psalmist describes the low state of his nation in terms of an exile into the
realm of the dead.

Psalm 45 (44)

This psalm is an epithalamium, that is, a song composed for a marriage in honor of the bride and groom. It is apparently a piece written for a marriage between an Israelite king and some foreign princess. Some have thought it refers to the wedding between Ahab of Israel and Jezebel, daughter of Ethbaal, king of Sidon (1 Kings 16:31); this, however, is far from certain and in fact no exact occasion or date can be assigned to the psalm with certainty. Basically, the psalm is divided into two parts; the first is addressed to the royal groom (verses 2-10); the second addresses the queenly bride (verses 11-17); the last verse is a brief prayer.

1 *For the director: On "the lilies . . . " A maskil of the sons of Korah. A song of love.*

2 My heart brims over with a joyful melody:
I will recite my masterpiece to the king.
May my tongue be the quill of a skillful scribe.

3 You are the handsomest among sons of men.
Kindness flows from your lips.

The Most High, the Truthful One, has blessed
you.
God has promised you prosperity forevermore.

4 Buckle your sword at your side.
May your majesty be victorious;
may your splendor make your conquest complete!

5 Ride on triumphant for the cause of truth,
defend the poor,
and may the deeds of your right hand win you
renown!

May your arrows be sharp!
6 May nations fall at your feet!
May the enemies of the king be stunned!

7 God, eternal and everlasting, has enthroned you.
May the scepter of your reign
be a scepter of equity!

8   May you love justice and hate wrongdoing,
    The Most High, the Truthful One, has anointed
        you.
    God, your God, has made you king.
    Your robes are perfumed with gladness:

9   your garments are all myrrh, sandalwood, and
        cinnamon.
    How many your palaces of ivory!
    How many there are to make you glad!

10   Royal women are appointed for your mansions,
    a queen on your right in gold of Ophir.

11   Pay heed, O daughter, listen and see:
    forget your people and your father's house.

12   The king will take you to himself,
    for he is now your sovereign
    and you must bow down before him.

13   A robe from Tyre is among your gifts.
    The wedding guests long to see your face.

14   "All glorious is her royal gown,
    woven skillfully with threads of gold!

15   Let the maiden bride be brought to the king;
    let her ladies-in-waiting approach with her.

16   Come, let her be brought
    with gladness and rejoicing!
    Let her enter the king's royal palace!"

17   In the place of your fathers
    let your sons now be:
    you will make them princes throughout the entire
        land.

18   May I make your name immortal,
    O Most High, O Truthful One.
    May peoples give you praise,
    O Eternal, Everlasting One.

Psalm 46 (45)

A hymn of confidence in the power and protection of the God who creates and watches over his holy people. This song praises God who overthrew the forces of chaos and calls upon him to continue to defeat every power that would undermine his holy city. Verse 11 is an answer from God to reassure the praying people that God will indeed persist in his course of providing fertility and richness to the land and turning back hostile forces that men hurl against his city and his shrine. The psalm was probably used at the fall festival of creation and covenant.

1 *For the director: a song of the sons of Korah; according to "The Maidens."*

2 O God, be our shelter and our stronghold,
   be ready to help in times of siege, O Everlasting
   One.

3 God, Most High and Truthful,
   we will not be afraid of the Dominion of Death
   or of the mountains being rocked
   into the heart of the sea.

4 We will not be afraid
   though its waters thunder and heave,
   though mountains rumble in its depths
   and its currents and channels stand in a heap.

5 God brings joy to his city—
   the Most High keeps his dwelling sacred.

6 God lives in that city
   and she will never be overthrown;
   God will come to her aid at break of day.

7 Nations may be in tumult, kingdoms may be
   shaken;
   when God speaks out, earth will grow faint.

8 Yahweh of power and might is with us!
   The God of Jacob is a refuge for us!

9 Come and see what Yahweh has done.
He gives the land its richness.

10 He drives the battles lines of our assailants
back to the edge of the world below.
He smashes the bow, splinters the spear,
sets the shields on fire.

11 "Be at rest, then, and know that I am God,
exalted over the nations, exalted over the earth."

12 Yahweh of power and might is with us!
The God of Jacob is a refuge for us!

Psalm 47 (46)

This psalm is apparently a hymn for the enthronement festival of Yahweh. It seems to have its origin in the northern kingdom of Israel for it calls the country "Pride of Jacob", as does Amos (cf. Amos 6:8 and 8:7) who prophesied in that kingdom. The psalm opens with acclamations for God who has subdued all the world (verses 1-5); then the poet announces that Yahweh has taken his throne in the shrine (verses 6-7); finally, the theme of the first verses is recalled and expanded (verses 8-10).

1   *For the director: a psalm of the sons of Korah.*

2   All you peoples, clap your hands!
     Raise a shout to God with a ringing cry!

3   Yahweh, the Most High, inspires awe,
     the great king rules over the earth.

4   He has prostrated nations under us
     and subdued peoples under our feet.

5   He chose our inheritance for us,
     the "Pride of Jacob," which he loves.

6   God has ascended amid acclamations;
     Yahweh has gone up to a flourish of trumpets.

7   Make music for God, make music for him.
     Make music for our king, make music for him.

8   God is king over the whole earth,
     so sing him a worthy song.

9   God has become king over the nations;
     God has seated himself on his throne.

10   Come together, nobles of the earth!
     The Mighty One of Abraham is God.
     Yes, God is the sovereign of the earth,
     highly to be exalted!

Psalm 48 (47)

This song of Zion is a hymn of praise to the Lord. It seems to be a song of victory after Jerusalem had been delivered from a coalition of foreign kings. The theme of the song is not necessarily any particular historical event. It was probably used to celebrate the victory of Yahweh over chaos and all other enemies, a victory commemorated at the fall festival.

1 *A song; a psalm of the sons of Korah.*

2 Great is Yahweh;
 worthy of all praise is the Mighty One,
 in the city of our God,
 on his holy mountain.

3 How lovely are its heights!
 It is the delight of all the earth.
 Mount Zion is the very dwelling of God,
 and the city of the great King.

4 God himself is her fortress,
 he is known to be her shield.

5 But kings were assembled against her,
 they were advancing as one man.

6 Then they looked and were struck with
  amazement;
 they were terrified and began quaking with fear.

7 They began to tremble,
 and started to writhe like a woman in labor,

8 and toss like the ships of Tarshish[a]
 when a hurricane from the east smashes them.

---

a Probably these were the largest ships known to the psalmist. They were cargo ships which hauled metal products from Tarshish, a place unknown, but probably to be identified with Spain or Sardinia.

9   All we had heard we have now seen with our own
       eyes,
    right here in the city of Yahweh of power and
       might,
    in the city of our God.
    God has made her foundations firm forever.

10   We are reflecting, O God, on your unfailing love,
    within your temple.

11   Your praise, O God, like your name
    reaches to the ends of the earth.
    Your right hand overflows with your victory;

12   Mount Zion is glad,
    and the towns of Judah dance for joy,
    because of the conquest you have made.

13   Hold a procession and walk all around Zion;
    count the number of her towers;

14   take note of her ramparts,
    mark her fortresses well.
    Then you will be able to tell the next generation:

15   "This God of ours—God forever and ever—
    he is the one who will guide us
    for all time to come."

Psalm 49 (48)

This poem, one of the most difficult to translate and understand in the entire psalter, seems to be a wisdom poem. Its language is ironic and its thought rather baffling. The author speaks of it as a "riddle" in verse 5, and so it remains. The general meaning of the psalm seems to be that life is brief, that riches cannot buy a reprieve from the grave, and that all, the wise and the foolish, ultimately will die. Yet verse 16 seems to express a hope of some deliverance or other for the psalmist, unless the author is quoting in satire the beliefs of those for whose benefit he is reciting his dire warnings. The poem is a stark reminder of the futility of attempts at pleasure and prosperity in this world, and hence provides incentive for Christian detachment.

1 *For the director: a psalm of the sons of Korah.*

2 Listen to these things, all you peoples;
   pay attention to them, all you inhabitants of earth,

3 common folk and high-born men,
   the wealthy as well as the needy.

4 My mouth would speak wise words;
   my heart would murmur insights.

5 I will turn my ear to a proverb;
   I will begin my riddle on a lyre.

6 Why should I be afraid on the day of deadly
         danger,
   when surrounded by the malice of those who
         slander me,

7 by those who trust in their riches
   and in their abundance of wealth make their
         boast?

8 Alas, a man can in no way redeem himself
   nor can he give God his own ransom.

9   Far too expensive is the ransom of his life;
     forever insufficient, what he is able to pay
10   to continue living and not see the Pit.[a]

11   If God looks at the wise, they die;
     if he gazes on fools, they perish at once,
     and leave others their riches.

12   Their graves are their homes forever,
     there they will dwell from age to age,
     though they had once acquired estates for
          themselves.

13   No, a man will not continue in his wealth;
     he is like the animals that cease to exist.

14   This is the destiny of those who possessed riches—
     the final end of those who pursued their own
          pleasure.

15   Like a flock of sheep they will be herded into
          Sheol.
     Death will be their shepherd.

     When they descend into his throat like a calf,
     their bodies will be eaten up by Sheol,
     consumed by the Devourer.

16   But God will redeem my soul;
     he will surely snatch me from the hand of Sheol.

17   Do not be envious if a man grows rich—
     if the glory of his house increases.

18   When he dies he will take nothing with him;
     his glory will not follow him,
19   though he worshipped himself while he lived.

     And though they praise you when your prosper,

---

a This translation follows that of Fr. Dahood (PAB, I, p. 295). The Hebrew
text is far from clear.

20 you will go to the company of your fathers,
   never more to see the light.

21 No, a man who is wealthy does not understand:
   he is like the animals that cease to exist.

Psalm 50 (49)

This psalm has been called a prophetic liturgy and is a poem which contains material that is familiar to us from the writings of the prophets. The poem takes the form of a dispute held by Yahweh against the worship without ethics that was a common temptation for ancient Israel, and for modern Christians as well. In a pattern reminiscent of Isaiah 1, the psalmist calls all creation to be his witness in his contention with his people. Then the people are reminded that the material elements of sacrifices were not what Yahweh was asking of them. Moral and ethical norms of conduct as well as true praise would merit rewards from the Lord. All of this seems to foreshadow the saying of Jesus that true worshippers will worship in spirit and truth.

1 *A psalm of Asaph.*

Yahweh, the God of gods, has spoken:
he has summoned the earth
from the rising of the sun to its setting.

2 From Zion, the perfection of beauty,
God has shown himself with radiance.

3 Our God is coming and he will not be silent.
A fire goes before him, consuming;
all around him, a violent storm is raging.

4 He summons the heavens down from above,
and the earth below,
to try his people:

5 "Assemble before me those who are loyal to me—
those who entered a covenant with me
and ratified it with a sacrifice."

6 The very heavens will announce his just claim:
that he is the God of fair judgment.

7 "Listen, my people, and I shall speak:
I shall testify against you, Israel;
I am God, your God.

8   It is not about your sacrifices
    that I am charging you,
    nor about your burnt-offerings
    which are continually before me.

9   I am not demanding bulls from your farms,
    nor bucks from your herds of goats.

10 To me belong all the creatures of the forest
    and all the beasts of the lofty mountains.

11 I know everything that flies in the hills;
    all that moves in the fields is in my sight.

12 Were I to get hungry, I would not tell you,
    for mine is the world and all that fills it.

13 Do I eat the flesh of bulls
    and drink the blood of bucks?

14 Make praise your sacrifice to God;
    keep your promises to the Most High.

15 Then call to me on the day of distress
    and I shall deliver you and make a feast for you."

16 But this is what God says to the evil man:
    "What business is it of yours to recite my laws,
    to review the terms of my covenant?

17 You are the one who hates my discipline
    and throws my words behind your back.

18 If you see a thief, you vie with him,
    and you throw in your lot
    with those who commit adultery.

19 With your mouth you forge evil
    and with your tongue you weld deceit together.

20 You sit down to speak against your brother,
    you malign the son of your own mother.

21 You did all these things. Was I to be silent?
You thought what is evil. Was I to be like you?

I am accusing you
and drawing up my case before your eyes.

22 Mark these things, you that forget God,
lest I begin to tear you in pieces
and there be no Rescuer.

23 For him who offers praise,
I shall give a feast;
for him who takes his stand on my path,
I shall pour a drink from the salvation of God."

Psalm 51 (50)

The fourth of the penitential psalms. It is very probable that this song originated as a liturgy of penance in the royal court. At all events, the psalm has a very spiritual character and a deep sensitivity about sin and guilt is evident to those who pray it. Many scholars think that verses 18 and 19 are a later liturgical additon to the original poem, and that verses 20 and 21 are a still later stanza, added after the Exile when the walls of Jerusalem lay in ruins. None of this is certain, however.

1 *For the director: a psalm of David.*

2 *When the prophet Nathan went to David, just as he himself had gone to Bathsheba.*

3 Have pity on me, O God, in your unfailing love;
   in the abundance of your compassion
   erase my rebellious deeds.

4 Wash my guilt away, over and over,
   and from my sin make me clean.

5 How well I know my rebellious acts,
   and my sin is ever before me.

6 Against you and you alone did I sin,
   and I did what you regard as evil.

   So, you are just in your sentence
   and blameless in your judgment.

7 In guilt itself was I born,
   and in sin my mother conceived me.

8 Truth pleases you more than cleverness;
   you teach wisdom rather than secrets of the
      occult.[a]

---

a The "secrets of the occult" are Canaanite magical practices, used by them to obtain favors from their gods. The psalmist wants no part of this.

9 Take my sin away
and I will be purer than splashing water;
wash me and I will be whiter than snow.

10 Let me hear songs of joy and happiness
and the bones you crushed will be overjoyed.

11 Turn your face away from my sins
and erase all my guilt.

12 Create a clean heart for me, O God,
and put a new and constant spirit in my breast.

13 Do not banish me from your presence;
do not remove your holy spirit from me.

14 Restore to me the joy of your deliverance
and uphold me with a generous spirit

15 that I may teach rebels your ways
and sinners to return to you.

16 Rescue me from the Land of Tears,
O God, my God;
O my Savior, let my tongue shout your generosity.

17 O Lord, open my lips,
and my mouth shall declare your praise.

18 Had it been sacrifice that pleased you,
I would surely have offered it,
but you would have none of that.

19 The most pleasing sacrifice is a contrite spirit:
a bruised and broken heart is something you will
not despise, O God.

20 In your goodness, be kind to Zion:
build up the walls of Jerusalem.

21 Then you will be pleased with the legal
sacrifices—
with burnt-offering and whole-offering;
then young bulls will be offered on your altar.

Psalm 52 (51)

A prophetic oracle against the wiles of idolaters. Scholars have long sought to find the exact genre of this poem, and the quest goes on. But the style of this psalm and its thoughts are similar to prophetic attacks on those unfaithful to Yahweh, including predictions of doom. The psalmist begins by denouncing the deceiver as a master of evil who boasts of covenant loyalty while undermining the covenant itself (verses 3-6). He utters a fearful curse on the perverter of God's people and predicts the taunting laughter that will follow his downfall (verses 7-9). Finally, speaking for the community, he proclaims his own fidelity and confidence in God's goodness to loyal men (verses 10-11).

1   *For the director: a maskil of David.*

2   *When Doeg, the Edomite, came and told Saul,
    "David has gone to the house of Ahimelech."*

3   O champion in evil, why is the unfailing love
        of God
    your boast all the day?

4   You scheme your evil desires;
    your tongue is like a sharp razor,
    you maker of deceitful idols!

5   You prefer bad to good,
    you prefer to deceive rather than to speak justly.

6   You love anything that causes harm,
    you deceitful tongue.

7   May God demolish you, crush you forever,
    sweep you out of your tent,
    root you up from the land of the living!

8   Just men will see it and be afraid.
    But then they will laugh and say:

9 "There is the man who did not make God his
        refuge;
    instead, he trusted in his own great wealth
    and in his mighty power to destroy."

10 But, like an olive tree
    flourishing in God's house,
    I trust in his unfailing love
    until eternity and beyond.

11 I will thank you forever
    because you have acted,
    and I will proclaim how good your name is—
    how good it is to those who are loyal to you.

Psalm 53 (52)

Psalm 53 is very nearly word for word the same as Psalm 14.
Among the very few differences between the two psalms is that
the present one speaks of God as "elohim", i.e., "God",
whereas the other uses the divine name "Yahweh". No fully
satisfactory reason can be given why the psalm appears twice
in the collection. Perhaps one is a northern variation on a
southern version which is found in Psalm 14.

1 *For the director: according to "mahalath."*
   A maskil of David.

2 The fool declares in his heart:
   "God has no power."
   Men are depraved, they commit outrageous acts,
       not one does anything good.

3 God looks down from heaven upon all men,
   to see if any are wise,
   if a single one is seeking God.

4 All are apostates;
   all alike are corrupt.
   Not one does anything good,
   not a single one.

5 Those idolaters who devour his people—
   will they not understand?
   It is God's grain, which they did not gather,
   that they are devouring.

6 They have formed a conspiracy,
   but their conspiracy did not endure,
   for God scattered the bones
   of those encamped against you.
   You had to endure humiliation
   but God has rejected them.

7 If only Israel's deliverance would come out of
      Zion!
  When God gives a good harvest to his people,
  then will Jacob rejoice and Israel be glad.

Psalm 54 (53)

Psalm 54 is the ritual prayer of a king. He is threatened by "barbarians" and "savages", who are either foreign enemies or rebellious vassals, or even subjects who long for a non-Israelite king as ruler. The king, however, trusts in Yahweh's covenant fidelity, whereby he is able to triumph in the end over his treacherous opponents.

1 *For the director: for strings; a maskil of David.*

2 *When the Ziphites came and told Saul:*
"David is in hiding with us."

3 Rescue me, O God, with your name,
and defend me with your might.

4 Hear my prayer, O God;
listen to the words I speak.

5 Barbarians have risen against me
and savage men seek my life.
They have not taken God for their guide.

6 But God is my helper.
My Sovereign is the support of my life.

7 He turned the evil back on those
who denounced me.[a]
In his fidelity he utterly destroyed them.

8 I will sacrifice to you for your generosity;
I will praise your name, Yahweh—
how good it is!

9 He rescued me from all my anguish,
and I gloated over the fall of my foes.

---

a Those who "denounce" the king are either foreign enemies or disgruntled subjects. Their opposition is regarded as taking the form of denunciations to their gods, or even to Yahweh, demanding the removal of Israel's king.

Psalm 55 (54)

Psalm 55 is the lament of an individual. It seems to be composed in the spirit and in the circumstances of Elijah, the prophet (cf. 1 Kings 19). Like Elijah this psalmist is surrounded by treacherous enemies; the language of this psalm suggests that the malice and evil of the enemies is idolatry. Like Elijah, the psalmist finds all his sustenance in Yahweh. Even in his violent curses on his enemies (verses 10, 16) the psalmist resembles the great prophet. Probably this psalm is a product of some holy man in the northern kingdom in a time when idolatry was prevalent to the extent that loyal worshippers of Yahweh went about in danger of their lives.

1. *For the director: for strings; a maskil of David.*

2 O God, listen to my prayer;
    do not feign ignorance of my plea for mercy.

3 Be attentive to me and answer me;
    come down at my lament.

4 I shiver at the voice of the enemy,
    at the stare of the wicked,
    because they hurl malice at me
    and denounce me to my face.

5 My heart is pounding in my breast
    and the terrors of death fall upon me.

6 Fear and trembling overcome me;
    shuddering overwhelms me.

7 I think:
    If only someone would give me wings like a dove,
    then I would fly away and come to rest.

8 Yes, I would flee far away:
    I would lodge in the wilderness—

9 I would hurry to my hideaway,
    my shelter from the raging wind and the
        hurricane.

10 O my Sovereign, destroy their deceitful tongues
   because I see violence and strife in the city.

11 Day and night they make their rounds,
   on the city walls are both malice and mischief.

12 From its heart come evil deeds;
   from its heart they do not depart,
   from its central square come oppression and
       dread.

13 It was not a foe who reproached me—
   I could have borne that.
   It was not an enemy who turned against me—
   I might have hid myself from him.

14 But, it was you, a man of my own kind,
   my familiar and intimate friend.

15 We had enjoyed each other's deep affection;
   in the house of God we had walked with the
       throng.

16 May death fall upon them,
   may they go down alive to Sheol,
   because malice is in their houses,
   and on their city square.

17 But I call to God and Yahweh will save me.

18 Evening and morning and high noon
   I complain and I moan,
   and the Redeemer listens to my voice.

19 He ransoms my life with abundance;
   he comes near to me
   even though many are against me.

20 God will hear and answer me:
   the Ancient One will send his reply.
   In him there is no vacillating,
   yet they will not reverence God.

21 My enemy raises his hands
against his companion;
he profanes his agreement.

22 His speech is smoother than cream,
but a plan of attack is in his heart.
His words are soothing like oil,
but they are drawn swords.

23 Your provider is Yahweh, Most High;
he is your benefactor who will sustain you.[a]
Never will he allow the just man to stumble.

24 You, O God,
will hurl them down to the foul pit;
men of idols and lying statues—
they will not live out half their days,
but I put my trust in you.

---

[a] The translation here follows Fr. Dahood (PAB, II, 29). The Hebrew text as
it stands reads: "Cast upon Yahweh your cares and he will sustain you."

Psalm 56 (55)

Psalm 56 is a poem of pre-exilic date. Its images suggest that it was the lament of an Israelite king surrounded by enemies who denounced him (vassals or subjects dissatisfied with his reign and his loyalty to God). They are depicted in the guise of stalking hunters (verses 3, 7) and attacking warriors (verse 10). The king again and again declares his confidence in God who will rescue him and regards his deliverance as nothing less than liberation from the realm of death.

1. *For the director: on "Yonath elom rehoqim"* ª; *a miktam of David, when the Philistines seized him in Gath.*

2 Have pity on me, O God,
   because men are hounding me.
   All day long they are hemming me in with
        their attacks.

3 Those who denounce me keep hounding me
        all day long.
   How many are those who fight against me!

4 O Most High, on the day I am afraid,
   I put my trust in you.

5 Listen, you who denounce me,
   I glory in God:

   I trust in God and will not be afraid.
   What can flesh do against me?

6 All day long those who denounce me cause me
        pain;
   all their schemes weigh heavily upon me.

ª The meaning of this phrase in Hebrew has successfully eluded all attempts at a meaningful translation.

7 They assemble with malice;
   they lurk in hiding,
   watching my footsteps to take my life.

8 Deliver us from evil!
   In your anger, O God,
   bring the peoples under your dominion!

9 Add up my moans yourself;
   enter my tears in your record,
   my sufferings in your account.

10 If my enemies draw back,
   retreating on the day I call,
   then I will know God is on my side.

11 Listen, you who denounce me,
   I glory in God;
   listen, you who denounce me,
   I glory in Yahweh.

12 I trust in God and will not be afraid.
   What can man do against me?

13 O God, Most High,
   I will keep my promises;
   I will offer my thanksgiving to you.

14 You have rescued my life from death,
   my feet from the place of banishment,
   so that I may walk before the face of God
   in the Field of Life.

Psalm 57 (56)

A royal psalm. Like Psalm 56 the present poem is a lament of a king, appealing to the divine covenant virtues, unfailing love and faithfulness (verse 4) to deliver him from the denunciation of his enemies. These foes are painted in the guise of dogs who track the king (verse 4), lions that terrify him (verse 5), and ingenious hunters who are intent on trapping him (verse 7). In the face of these dangers, the king's heart is hopeful, and he acknowledges that the promises of his God surpass every mortal peril (verses 8-12).

1 *For the director: "Do not destroy . . ."; a miktam of*
 David when he was fleeing from Saul into the cave.

2 Have pity on me, O God, have pity on me,
 because my soul takes refuge in you.

 In the shadow of your wings I take refuge
 until the calamity passes by.

3 I call to God, the Most High,
 to God, the Avenger, the Most High.

4 He will answer from heaven.
 He will save me
 from the abuse of those who hound me.
 God will send his unfailing love
 and his faithfulness.

5 My soul is among lions.
 I must lie among beasts who roar at men.
 Their teeth are spears and arrows,
 their tongues are sharpened swords.

6 You tower above the heavens, O God;
 high above all the earth is your glory!

7 They have spread a net for my feet,
 a noose for my neck.
 They have dug a pit in front of me.
 May they fall into it themselves!

8 My heart is confident, O God,
   my heart is confident;
   I will sing and play music.

9 Awake, my heart!
   Awake, harp and lyre!
   I would awaken the dawn!

10 I would thank you, O my Sovereign, among the
       peoples;
   I would play music to you among the nations!

11 High as the heavens is your unfailing love,
   high as the clouds your faithfulness.

12 You tower above the heavens, O God;
   high above all the earth is your glory!

Psalm 58 (57)

In many ways Psalm 58 is unique. It resembles the threats hurled by some of the prophets against those unjust powers that perpetrate social injustices in the land. Just who these powers are, who are addressed in this psalm, is disputed. Some scholars think that false gods are the addressees; others that unjust judges, idolatrous officials, are the culprits. Perhaps the psalmist had both categories in mind; the belief that evil officials were the allies of idols would not have been wide of the mark in the thinking of the prophets. At all events the psalmist prays that those who further the cause of evil in the world be disarmed, that their power be overcome and that just men finally see their hopes vindicated.

1   *For the director: "Do not destroy . . ."; a miktam*
    of David.

2   Epert counsellors and powerful leaders,
       if only your verdicts were just!
    If only you would judge the lowly with fairness.

3   But instead, you act with malice in your hearts;
       you weigh out your decisions with hands stained
          by lawlessness.

4   Evil men are loathsome from the time they are
          born.
    Speakers for lying idols are wayward from the
          womb.

5   They have a venom like the venom of a viper—
       a deaf adder that stops up its ears:

6   an adder that will not listen
       to the voice of the charmer,
    the clever charmer who casts spells.

7   O God, pull the teeth from their mouths;
       smash the fangs of the lions' cubs, Yahweh.

8   Let them ebb like water that swiftly runs away.
    If the enemy shoots arrows let their flight not be
        true.

9   Like a man consumed with disease, may he pass
        away;
    like a stillborn child of a woman,
    may he never see the sun.

10 May God root them out like a thornbush
    before they begin to grow;
    may he blow them away like thistles in a storm.

11 The just man will rejoice when he sees his rescue;
    he will wash the evil man's blood from his feet.

12 Men will say:
    "Yes, the just man does have a reward.
    Yes, there is a God who holds judgment on the
        earth."

Psalm 59 (58)

A royal lament. The king prays in this psalm to be liberated from his perfidious enemies. Their identity is not certain. They may be treacherous subjects or disloyal vassals. They are men who hold to idols instead of to God, and they stalk the king's domain like hungry jackals or wild dogs, those well-known denizens of villages in the Near East. The king, though endangered, maintains fealty to Yahweh, and prays that his suzerain will call the lurking foes to account and pass sentence on them so that loyal subjects will be impressed anew with the justice of the Lord.

1 *For the director: "Do not destroy . . ."; a miktam of*
   David; when Saul gave orders to keep his house
   under surveillance in order to kill him.

2 Deliver me from my foes, O God;
   secure me against those who attack me.

3 Deliver me from idolaters;
   save me from men who worship idols.

4 See, they are laying an ambush for me;
   powerful men are assembling against me.

5 For no transgression or sin of mine, Yahweh,
   for no iniquity of mine
   they are advancing and taking positions for battle.

6 Arise when I meet them and see for yourself,
   Yahweh, God of power and might, God of Israel.
   Awake to bring vengeance on all the nations,
   show no pity to those who are evil and
      treacherous.

7 They wait for evening,
   then growl like dogs and prowl around the city.

8 Behold, evil spews from their mouths,
   swords come from their lips,
   and they say: "Who is listening?"

9   But you will laugh at them, Yahweh;
    you will scoff at all the nations.

10 A fortress is my God!
    I am guarded well, because God is my bulwark—

11 a rampart is my God.
    God will go before me;
    he will let me gloat over those who denounce me.

12 O God, slay them
    so my people will not grow faint-hearted.

    Drive them reeling from your towers
    and force them down.^a
    Our shield is the Lord, our Sovereign.

13 Let them be caught by the sin of their mouths
    and the words of their lips.
    Let them be charged with pride and perjury and
        lying.^b

14 Exterminate them in your burning anger,
    exterminate them, annihilate them;
    then let them know that God rules
    from Jacob to the edges of the earth.

15 They wait for evening,
    then growl like dogs and prowl around the city.

16 They go scavenging about;
    if they are not filled, they remain through the night

---

^a The psalmist is praying in this verse that his enemies be driven down to the
realm of the dead—which is not necessarily to be understood literally. He
may mean that their might be destroyed and that they be defenseless.

^b The crimes for which the enemies are to be indicted are all concerned with
the covenant which they have violated; they have turned their backs on
Yahweh and his king.

17 But I will sing of your might;
every morning I will shout of your constancy.

You are a bulwark to me,
a refuge on the day I am besieged.

18 A fortress is my God!
I am guarded well,
because God is my bulwark—my rampart is my
God.

Psalm 60 (59)

A national lament. Though this psalm is difficult to date exactly, and is often classed as post-exilic, a good case can be made for a pre-exilic dating. Despite the title in verses 1 and 2, no particular defeat has to be regarded as the occasion for this psalm. It was probably used as a prayer for the on-going victory and prosperity of the nation. The poet tends to conceive of the country as it was in the days of the united monarchy in the time of David and Solomon. Beginning with a plaint of defeat and abandonment on God's part, the psalmist prays for victory in verses 6 and 7. Verses 8 to 10 are an example of a priestly oracle pronounced from a shrine in which the whole nation is declared to be the property and, indeed, the very armor of God. Verses 11 to 14 are spoken in the person of the king who speaks with great hope for the future provided he is assured the divine assistance.

1   *For the director: on "Shusan Eduth";*
     a miktam of David, to be taught.

2   *After he had struggled with Aram Naharaim and*
     Aram Sobah, and Joab returned and struck Edom
     in the Valley of Salt, killing twelve thousand of
     them.

The Lament for Defeat

3   You were angry with us, O God,
     and you burst out of our ranks;
     you were enraged and you turned away from us.

4   You shook the land and severed it into fragments;
     weak and broken, how it did shudder!

5   You forced your people to drain a mug,
     gave us a wine to drink that made us reel.[a]

---

[a] The poisoned cup of the wrath of God was a common metaphor in the prophetic writings. Jesus asked that he might pass up this awful draught in his prayer to the Father in the Garden of Gethsemani (cf. Mark 14:36).

6 Give a banner to those who fear you
so they may rally to it when the archers attack.

7 Let your right hand bring us victory,
so that your beloved people may be rescued.

The Divine Oracle

8 God made a pronouncement from his sanctuary:
"Gladly I take Shechem[b] for my portion
and measure off the Valley of Succoth.[c]

9 To me falls Gilead,[d] Manasseh[e] falls to me;
Ephraim[f] is my helmet, Judah[g] my mace.

10 Moab[h] is my washbowl,
Edom the property I claim when I plant my boot.
Over Philistia I shout in victory."

The King's Final Prayer

11 Who will bring me to Petra?
Who will set me on Edom's throne?

12 Will you, O God, stay angry at us
and never again march out with our armies?

13 Bring us aid against those who assail us,
because there is no hope for deliverance by man.

14 With God we will do mighty deeds;
he himself will trample our adversaries.

---

b The capital of the northern kingdom.
c A valley east of the Jordan.
d A fertile area in the Trans-Jordan.
e The largest of the northern tribes.
f The most powerful of the northern tribes.
g Judah was the principal southern tribe.
h Moah, Edom, and Philistia were political vassals of Israel. Petra was the capital of Edom, inaccessible and difficult to capture.

Psalm 61 (60)

Psalm 61 is a royal lament. The king is the speaker—the change to the third person in verses 7 and 8 is merely ancient Near Eastern court style—and he prays as if from a situation of great anguish (from the rim of the realm of the dead in verse 3). He prays for prosperity, daring to ask for the favor of living with God in his heavenly palace permanently. This may be simply a request for longevity and a happy lot or it may have some more mystical undertone. Some authors have considered the intent of the psalmist as a bid for everlasting life in heaven, but the evidence for this seems too slim to justify such a conclusion.

1   *For the director: for strings; of David.*

2   Hear, O God, my ringing cry!
    Listen to my prayer.

3   From the edge of the world below
    I call to you with fainting heart.

    Lead me from here to the lofty mountain.

4   Be a refuge for me—
    a tower of strength against the foe.

5   Let me be a guest in your everlasting tent;
    let me find refuge in the shelter of your wings.

6   If only you, O God, would listen to my promises
    and give me what you give to those who reverence
        your name.

7   Add many days to the days of the king.
    May his years be like many generations.

8   May he sit enthroned forever
    before the face of God.
    May unfailing love and faithfulness
    be appointed his sentries.

9   Then I will always play music to your name,
    fulfilling my promises day after day.

Psalm 62 (61)

There is little agreement among scholars as to the origin of this psalm. Its principal message is implicit trust in God. The psalmist is confronted with enemies, who would force him to put his trust elsewhere than in God (verses 4-5). But the poet places his confidence in God alone and encourages all the people to do the same (verses 6-12). Because he addresses people in general in this way it has been surmised that the psalmist is a king or wisdom teacher or prophet.

1   *For the director: according to "Jeduthun"; a psalm of David.*

2   The Most High alone is my citadel;
from him, O my soul, comes my victory.

3   He alone is my mountain, my victory, my
       rampart.
I will not go on stumbling.

4   How long will you speak against a man?
How long will all of you push him down
as if he were a leaning wall or a sagging fence?

5   They plan only deceit;
they enjoy the lies that bring destruction.
They bless from their mouths,
but in their hearts they curse.

6   My citadel is God alone;
from him, O my soul, comes my hope.

7   He alone is my mountain, my victory, my
       rampart.
I will not stumble.

8   God, the Most High, is my Savior;
my Glorious One is my mountain-fortress.
God himself is my refuge.

9 Trust in him, people, at all times;
  pour out your hearts to him.
  God is a refuge for us.

10 Common men are only a vapor—
  men of high rank, a delusion:
  on the scale they are lighter than leaves;
  all together they weigh less than a vapor.

11 Put no trust in extortion and cheating;
  place no empty hopes in wealth.
  When God speaks, repent from your heart.

12 God spoke once and I heard two things:
  Power belongs to God,
  and faithfulness is yours as well, O Sovereign.
  You repay each person according to his deeds.

Psalm 63 (62)

A royal psalm of trust. Using the language of intimacy and complete confidence, a king requests help and prosperity from God. Verses 2-9 declare the psalmist's love and desire for the divine presence and the divine assistance. Verses 10-12 express the confident hope that the king's enemies who trust in other gods will become like battle casualties—left on the field to become food for scavengers, while those who are loyal to God and king will prosper.

1   *A psalm of David, while he was in the wilderness of Judah.*

2   At daybreak I long for you, O God, my God.
    How thirsty is my soul for you!
    My body pines for you
        more than ground that is parched and dry and
            waterless.

3   Let me look upon you in your sanctuary;
    let me see your power and your glory.

4   Your unfailing love is sweeter than life!
    Let my lips proclaim you!

5   Let me go on blessing you throughout my life!
    Let me lift up my hands in your name!

6   Let my soul be filled
        as though with cream and juicy meat!
    Let me praise you as I cry out for joy!

7   When I think of you as I lie in bed,
        when I ponder on you as I watch through the
            night,

8   I think: "If only you would be my help,
        if only I might find refuge
            in the shadow of your wings.

9   Let my soul cling tightly to you,
        and your right hand hold me fast."

[133]

10 Those who seek my life to destroy it
   will go into the depths of the world below.

11 They will be struck by Death with the edge of the
       sword;
   they will become carrion for jackals.

12 But the king will rejoice in God.
   All who make their oaths by him will glory,
   but the mouths of those who speak for lying idols
       will be silenced.

Psalm 64 (63)

A prophetic lament against idolatry. The psalmist appeals to God to save him from inimical and godless men (verses 3-4). He describes the wiles of idolaters, men whose loose beliefs permit them to ignore the law and ensnare many with promises of easy prosperity (verses 5-6). But the poet is confident that God's all-seeing providence will find out their deeds and eventually bring them to open and final disgrace (verses 7-10). The poem ends with a word of encouragement for just men: let them find joy and refuge in Yahweh (verse 11).

1 *For the director: a psalm of David.*

2 Listen, O God, to my voice, to my lament:
protect my life from the enemy I dread.

3 Hide me from the assembly of the malicious,
from the noisy crowd of the idol worshippers:

4 they sharpen their tongues like swords
and aim their venomous words like arrows.

5 They shoot at the sincere from ambush—
they shoot suddenly, and have no fear.

6 They are firmly agreed on using deadly poison,
they discuss how they will lay the snares.
They say: "Who will see us?

7 Who will discover our perfect plan?"
The Searcher will probe
the innermost thoughts of man—
even the depths of his heart!

8 God will shoot an arrow
and sudden will be the blow they receive!

9 They will stumble over their own intrigues.
Everyone who looks upon them will be shaken:

10 every man will be afraid!
They will relate God's actions
and understand what he has done.

[135]

11 Let all the just be glad in Yahweh
    and run to him for refuge!
    Let all of upright heart praise him!

Psalm 65 (64)

A prayer for rain and for a bountiful harvest. Psalm 65 begins with a brief expression of penance for sins committed (verses 2-5). Such acts of penance are still preserved in the cycle of the autumn feasts in the Jewish liturgical year; a "Day of Atonement" is held before the new year's rains begin. Verses 6-14 recall the original wonder of creation, when God overcame the forces of chaos and made the world a fit place for people to live, and then express prayers that the coming year be one of rich crops and abundant prosperity.

1 *For the director: a psalm of David; a song.*

2 Praise to you in the great citadel[a]—
   to you, O God, who are on Zion.
   Let the promises made to you be kept—
   to you (3), the One who listens to prayer.

   To you all men bring (4) their guilty deeds—
   and our acts of rebellion have been beyond
         numbering.
   Forgive us all of them.

5 How happy the man you choose
   and bring to your presence to dwell in your court!
   Fill us with the beauty of your house
   and the holiness of your temple.

6 Hear us, O God, our Savior—
   you are awesome in judging,
      quieting all the ends of the earth and of the
         distant sea.

7 He made the mountains firm by his power
   because he was clothed with strength.

---

a "The great citadel": both the celestial dwelling of God, and its earthly counterpart, the temple.

[137]

8   He calmed the roaring of the seas,
    the roaring of the breakers,
    and the raging of the peoples.

9   While those who dwell at the ends of the earth
    stood dazed at your wonders,
    the sunrise and sunset shouted for joy.

10 Visit the earth—make her skip for joy.
    Bring down showers; make her rich.
    Let the divine watercourse be full.

    Prepare her grain, yes, make her ready;
11 drench her furrows, soak her ridges;
    soften her with showers, bless her first shoots.

12 Crown the mountains with your blessed rain,
    and may your meadows be lush with grass.

13 May the open pastures abound with richness,
    and attire the hills with rejoicing.

14 May the draws be decked with sheep,
    and the valleys be garbed with grain.
    May they shout for joy and break into song!

Psalm 66 (65)

A national hymn of thanksgiving. Many commentators regard
this psalm as a composite consisting of two poems: verses 1 to
12 (a national thanksgiving); and verses 13 to 20 (a personal
thanksgiving). However, if the whole be thought of as a song to
be recited in the person of a king or prominent leader of the
community who speaks for all, the difficulties of the commentators at least partially evaporate. This is not to say that
everything about this psalm is easily understandable. While it is
clear that verses 1 to 12 represent a joyous song of gratitude on
the part of the community, it is not entirely clear why a
celebration is being held. Verse 6 seems to be speaking of the
exodus from Egypt, but verse 7 is hard to explain if that is the
case. It seems best to regard the whole psalm as an expression
of the community's joy over God's care and providence in
rescuing his people from some calamity whose exact nature is
no longer known to us.

1 *For the director: a psalm, a song.*

   Shout to God for joy, all the land!
2 Sing his glorious name;
   recount his glorious praise!

3 Make this declaration:
   "Because of your works,
   how admirable you are, O God!
   Because of the greatness of your power
   your enemies fawn before you.

4 All the land worships you;
   it sings hymns in your honor
   and chants your name."

5 Come and see the works of God.
   How admirable you are for your marvels toward
        the lowly!

6 He changed the sea into dry land
   and they crossed the river on foot.
   Let us be glad in him.

7   He reigns from his everlasting fortress.
       His eyes watch the nations closely
       so no upstarts can rebel against him.

8   O peoples, praise our God!
       Make it be heard—the sound of his praise!

9   He placed us among the living
       and did not put our feet into the mire of death.

10   Yet you tested us, O God,
       and refined us as silver is refined.

11   You brought us into the trackless waste
       and made ulcers form on our thighs.

12   You made illness master over us.
       We went through fire and water.
       Then you guided us out to prosperity.

13   I will enter your house with burnt-offerings;
       I will fulfill my promises to you—

14   the promises that I deliberately made
       when I was in anguish.

15   I will make burnt-offerings of calves
       and the smoke of rams.
       I will prepare an ox and goats.

16   Come, all of you who reverence God.
       Listen and I will recount what he did for me.

17   I called him with my voice,
       and there was praise on my tongue.

18   Had I been conscious of idolatry in my heart,
       my Sovereign would not have listened.

19   But God did listen
       and paid attention to my voice when I prayed.

20   Blessed be God!
       He has not denied me my request
       or his unfailing love.

Psalm 67 (66)

A prayer for prosperity, particularly for plentiful rainfall and a good harvest. Like his victory over the powers of chaos at the world's beginning, so God's conquest of the evil forces of drought and starvation is the object of praise in ancient Israel. The psalmist here begins his prayer with a request for rain: May God come to us (verse 2). The ancients believed that drought was caused by God's absence from the land. Verses 3 to 6 express the belief in the coming triumph of God over all the earth. His annual victories over the forces of chaos, death and drought prepare for his final conquest when all the earth will be at last subject to him openly. Verses 7 and 8 sum up the psalm with a prayer for prosperity and an Old Testament expression of the thought of Jesus: Thy kingdom come.

1 *For the director: for strings; a psalm; a song.*

2 May God have pity on us and bless us!
    May he look on us kindly and may he come to us!

3 May your reign then be recognized on earth,
    and your victory among all the nations!

4 The peoples will praise you, O God;
    the peoples will praise you all together.

5 The peoples will be glad and shout for joy,
    because you act as judge.
    You will lead the nations to the level ground,
    and the peoples into the land.

6 The peoples will praise you, O God;
    the peoples will praise you all together.

7 May the earth yield its produce!
    May God, our God, bless us!

8 May God bless us,
    and may all the ends of the earth
    have reverence for him!

Psalm 68 (67)

The bewildering imagery and the confusing transitions between sections within this psalm make it difficult to assign a genre to Psalm 68. It is generally agreed that it is a hymn and a very ancient one. At least some lines of it go back to the age of the Judges, though in its final form it must have been completed after the foundation of the Davidic monarchy. While no particular historical event can be pointed to as the occasion of the composition of this poem, it is not unlikely that traditions of the exodus underlay the first 11 verses of this psalm. Perhaps God's assistance in the age of the Judges inspired verses 12 to 18. Verses 19 to 24 praise Yahweh for his defeat of the monsters of chaos. Verses 25 to 36 sound as if they had their origin in a procession of victory at the Jerusalem temple in the time of the united monarchy, that is, the age of David and Solomon. But it must be confessed that most of what is said about Psalm 68 lies in the realm of conjecture. What is certain is that the psalm is a hymn celebrating the power and the victories of the Lord on behalf of his people.

1 *For the director: a psalm of David; a song.*

2 When God rises up, his foes disperse;
his enemies flee before him.

3 Like smoke that is driven about,
they are driven about;
as wax runs before fire,
so the wicked disappear before God.

4 But the just will be glad
and leap with joy at the sight of God;
they will be jubilant and overjoyed.

5 Sing, O gods; play hymns, O heavens;
pave the road for the cloud-rider.
Delight in Yahweh! Leap for joy in his presence!

6 A Father of orphans, an Advocate for widows is
God
from his holy dwelling.

7 It was God who gave the solitaries a home[a]
and led prisoners out into freedom with songs of
joy,
but rebellious men found their final dwelling
was the wasteland.

8 O God,
when you went out at the head of your people,
when you advanced into the desert,

9 the earth began to quake.
The heavens themselves poured rain down
at the sight of God—the God of Sinai,
at the sight of God—the God of Israel.

10 Give an abundant rainfall, O God;
restore your heritage and your dominion.

11 Provide for your household that dwells in it;
restore its inhabitants with plentiful rain.

12 The Sovereign Lord gives the command—
its heralds are a mighty army.

13 They bow down—the kings of armies bow down!
The pastures of our homeland share the spoils.

14 While you dwelt among the sheepfolds,
Israel's wings, like a dove's, were covered with
silver,
her pinions with the pale yellow sheen of gold.[b]

15 While God, the Almighty,
drove the kings away from her,
she grew whiter than the snow on Mount Zalmon.

16 O mighty range, Mount Bashan!
O Mount Bashan, range of many peaks!

a Possibly this "home" is Palestine.
b In other words, Yahweh gave Israel the booty of victory though they
themselves dwelt in a state of peaceful prosperity.

17   Why, O range of many peaks, do you squint with
         envy
     at the mountain on which God chose to dwell,
     where Yahweh will live, yes live forever?

18   The chariots of God are twice ten thousand;
     thousands are the archers of the Lord
     who created Sinai as his sanctuary.

19   You ascended the heights, you took prisoners
     and accepted tribute from their hands—
     but Yahweh God has given the rebellious ones
         their final dwelling.[c]

20   Blest be the Sovereign Lord, day after day!
     God, our Savior, removes oppression from us.

21   Our God is a God who saves us,
     escape from death is in the power of Yahweh, our
         Sovereign.

22   Yes, God struck the heads of his enemies;
     he split their skulls
     when he marched out from his heaven.

23   The Sovereign Lord made this declaration:
     "I stifled the primeval serpent
     and muzzled the depths of the sea."

24   So your foot wallowed in their blood
     and the tongues of your dogs had their share of
         your foes.

25   Now see the procession of God—
     the procession of my God and King from his
         sanctuary!

c Verses 19-24 deal with the great victory of Yahweh over the forces of chaos.

26 The singers come first, the musicians bring up the
          rear,
    and, in the middle, the girls tapping their
          tambourines.

27 Bless God in the assembly—
    praise Yahweh in the convocation of Israel!

28 Benjamin the youngest—there he is in the lead;
    then Judah's officials, a throng of them;
    the leaders of Zebulun and the authorities of
          Naphtali.

29 Send out your own strength, O God;
    make firm what you have built for us.

30 Have kings bring you presents
    for your temple above Jerusalem.

31 Rebuke Egypt, the crocodile
    that lives among the reeds,
    and their herd of buffalo-generals and calf-armies.

    They trampled on peoples out of lust for silver,
    scattered peoples and found their pleasure in
          battle.

32 Let Egyptian merchants bring blue cloth
    and Sudan hasten with its wares to God.

33 Sing, O kings of the earth!
    Sing, O gods, your hymns to the Sovereign Lord!

34 Listen! the One who rides on his heavens,
    the primordial heavens,
    speaks with a thunder, his voice of power.

35 Give praise to God, the Most High of Israel;
    his majesty and his power are beyond the clouds.

36 More awesome is God than his sanctuary.
    Yes, he is the God of Israel,
    and he gives power and strength.
    O people, praise God!

Psalm 69 (68)

The lament of an individual, who may be a king. Psalm 69 resembles Psalm 22, in that both psalms begin with a lengthy lament and end on a note of thanksgiving. Verses 36 and 37, which pray for the deliverance of Judah and hence may be post-exilic, are regarded by some scholars as a later addition. The enemies of the psalmist are not identifiable, though they are in league with the forces of Death.

1 *For the director: on "Lilies . . ."; of David.*

2 Save me, O God,
because the waters have come up to my neck.

3 I have sunk into the mire of the Abyss[a]
and there is no foothold.

I have entered the Deepest Waters
and the Whirlpool is pulling me down.

4 I am tired of calling out;
my throat is dry;
my vision is blurred, O God, from watching so
long.

5 I have more lying enemies than hairs on my
head—
my deceitful foes outnumber them.
Must I restore what I did not take as plunder?[b]

6 O God, you know my foolish conduct;
my guilty deeds are not concealed from you.

---

[a] "The Abyss", "the Deepest Waters", "the Whirlpool": three poetic names for the realm of the dead.
[b] The psalmist has been charged with banditry. If he was a king it may be that his vassals have accused him of oppression.

7   Do not let those who wait for you
    be disgraced because of me,
    O my Master, Lord of power and might;
    do not let those who seek you be humiliated
    on my account, O God of Israel.

8   Because of you, I have endured disgrace;
    humiliation has been all over my face.

9   I have become a stranger to my brothers,
    an outsider to the sons of my own mother.

10 Yes, the hatred for your house^c
    turned on me and devoured me;
    the insults they hurl against you have fallen on
        me.

11 I afflicted my very soul while I fasted,
    but it brought me only reproach.

12 I made sackcloth my clothing
    but they made a jest of me.

13 The revellers and drunkards
    compose taunting songs about me.

14 Meanwhile I am praying to you.
    Yahweh, be pleased with me now.
    In the immensity of your unfailing love, O God,
    answer me.

    In your faithfulness to save
15 deliver me from the Mire and do not let me sink.
    Let me escape from Death, my Enemy,
    and from the Deepest Waters.

16 Do not let the Whirlpool deluge me,
    nor the Abyss swallow me up,
    nor the Pit close its mouth over me.

c The enemies hate the Lord's house, i.e., the temple. Hence they hate the
psalmist who is in league with the Lord.

17   Answer me, Yahweh,
     because your unfailing love is kind.
     In the abundance of your tenderness
     turn your face toward me.

18   Do not turn your face from your servant:
     answer me now because I am in anguish!

19   Come near to me and redeem me—
     ransom me from the domain of my Enemy.

20   You know my disgrace;
     my humiliation and my shame stand in your sight.

21   Insults have made my resolution weak;
     faintness is breaking my heart.

     I have been looking for someone to console me,
     but there is no one—
     for someone to comfort me,
     but I have found no one.

22   They put poison in my food,
     and when I was thirsty,
     they gave me vinegar to drink.

23   Let their own table be a trap for them,
     and even their companions, a snare.

24   May their vision be too blurred for them to see,
     their legs too shaky for them to stand!

25   Pour out your anger over them;
     let the fury of your rage overtake them.

26   May their encampment be desolate
     and let no one dwell in their tents,

27   because they persecuted the one you had struck
     and exaggerated about the one you had wounded!

28   Charge them with crime after crime
     and do not let them enter the meadow of life.

29   Let them be erased from the book of the living;
     may they not be registered among the just!

30   I am afflicted and grieved;
     may God's own deliverance make me secure

31   so I can praise the name of God in song
     and give glory to him with thanksgiving!

32   That will be more pleasing to Yahweh than a bull
     or an ox with horn and hoof.

33   Look at this, you downtrodden;
     rejoice, you that seek God:

34   May it rejoice your heart that God hears the
         poor,
     that Yahweh does not despise those
     who have committed themselves to him.

35   Let heaven and earth praise him,
     the seas and everything that moves about in
         them.

36   Surely God will rescue Zion
     and rebuild the cities of Judah,
     and those exiled from it will return there.

37   The descendants of his servants will inherit it;
     those who love his name will dwell in it.

Psalm 70 (69)

Psalm 70 is nearly identical with Psalm 40:14-18. It is unknown whether the present psalm was originally an independent composition inserted into Psalm 40 or whether Psalm 70 was removed from the larger work and used as a separate piece. As it stands alone it is a brief individual lament that pleads for a speedy rescue from the taunts of enemies.

1 *For the director: of David; for remembrance.*

2 O God, come to my rescue!
  Yahweh, come quickly to help me!

3 Let those who seek my life
  be humiliated and disgraced.

4 Let those who would enjoy my misfortunes
  shrink back in shame.

5 Let them be turned back
  and be astonished at their own defeat—
  those who hurl jeers at me.

  May all who seek you
  rejoice and be glad because of you.
  Let those who love your deliverance
  always say: "Great is God."

6 I am afflicted and poor.
  O God, hurry to me!
  My Help and my Rescue are you, my God,
  do not delay!

Psalm 71 (70)

The lament of a prominent person, perhaps a king. The striking note of this psalm is the apparent age of the psalmist. The prayer seems to be the supplication of an old man who has always trusted in the Lord. Now, in his old age, he is faced with fresh troubles and he turns to the God who has always been his protector. As he anticipates the divine assistance he concludes his prayer with the promise of joyful sacrifices.

1 In you, Yahweh, I have trusted;
   do not let me be disgraced, O Eternal One!

2 In your justice, rescue me and deliver me;
   turn your ear to me and save me.

3 Be my mountain to help me,
   always be ready to receive me;
   decree my deliverance
   because you are my mountain fastness, my
        fortress.

4 Rescue me, O God, from the hands of the wicked,
   from the grasp of the criminal and oppressor,

5 because you, my Sovereign Lord, have been my
        hope
   and my trust, O Yahweh, from my youth.

6 I have leaned on you from the womb;
   you have sustained me
   since I was at my mother's bosom.
   My boast has always been of you.

7 I have been like a target for archers,
   but you have been my mighty shelter.

8 My mouth is full of your praises,
   of your splendor all the day long.

9 Do not throw me out in my old age;
   do not abandon me when my vigor wanes.

[151]

10 My enemies spy on me—
    and those who watch my life consult together.

11 They say: "God has deserted him!
    Pursue him! Apprehend him!
    There is no one to rescue him!"

12 O God, do not be far from me!
    O God, come quickly to help me.

13 Let those who slander me
    be brought to shame and humiliation;
    let those who wish me evil
    be covered with disgrace and abuse.

14 I will always be hopeful.
    I will praise you more and more.

15 How I wish to relate your deeds of justice
    and your saving acts all the day long,
    though how to count them is beyond me.

16 I will go into your mighty house, O Sovereign
        Lord,
    I will recall your justice, Yahweh—yours alone.

17 O God, you have been teaching me since my
        youth
    and up to now I have been proclaiming your
        marvels.

18 So, even in old age and gray hair,
    O God, do not desert me
    until I proclaim your might before all the
        assembly
    and to everyone who enters your mighty house.

19 Your generosity, O God, is high as the heavens!
    What great things you have done!
    O God, who is like you?

20 Though you have made me see much anguish and
strife and evil,
you will restore me, make me live,
and bring me up again from the depths of the
earth.

21 Invest my animal sacrifices with value;
enfold me with your comfort.

22 I will praise you on the harp;
I will play to you on the lyre,
Holy One of Israel.

23 I will shout for joy and sing praise to you
with all my soul—which you have redeemed.

24 All day long I will reflect on your generosity.
How they have been humiliated,
how they have been disgraced—
those who seek to do away with me!

Psalm 72 (71)

A prayer for the king. Psalm 72 must have been used either on the occasion of a coronation or on the anniversary of the king's accession to the throne. Despite the fact that the Hebrew text includes the notation at the beginning "of Solomon", there is reason to believe that this psalm originated in the northern kingdom of Israel. The ideal of the kingship expressed here seems to belong to the north rather than to Jerusalem. The psalmist, who may be a priest or a prophet, prays that the king will be endowed with divine qualities (verses 1-2); he prays for prosperity in his reign (verses 3-7); he asks that his rule will be both famed and effective over many Gentiles (verses 8-11). Then, in verses 12 to 14 he lists the conditions necessary for the divine blessings on the king. The blessings themselves are then expressed (verses 15-17). The last two verses are a doxology indicating that the second book of the psalter, as the Hebrew text arranges it, is complete.

1   *Of Solomon.*

   O God, endow the king with your judgment,
   and the king's son with your justice,

2   that he may govern your people with justice,
   and your oppressed ones with judgment.

3   May the mountains bear your people peace
   and the hills, justice.

4   May he bring about justice to those
   who are oppressed among the people;
   may he deliver the children of the poor
   and crush the extortioner.

5   May he reverence you as long as there is a sun,
   and until the moon passes away,
   generation after generation.

6   May he be like rain falling on dry stubble,
   like showers on parched land.

7   May the just man thrive in his days:
   may prosperity abound until the moon is no more.

8   May his sovereignty extend from sea to sea
    and from the River[a] to the ends of the earth.

9   May the Bedouin bow down before him,
    and may his enemies taste the Mud of the world
      below.

10   May the kings of Tarshish[b] and the islands
      pay him tribute,
    and the kings of Sheba[c] and Arabia offer him
      gifts.

11   May all kings prostrate themselves before him;
    may all the nations become his slaves.

12   If he rescues the poor man when he cries for
      help,
    and the needy man when he has no one to help
      him;

13   if he has pity on the needy and the lowly,
    and saves the lives of the poor;

14   if he redeems their lives from oppression and
      violence
    and removes the idols from their sight—

15   then long may he live!
    May the gold of Sheba be given him!
    May prayer be offered for him perpetually.
    May he be blessed all the day long.

16   May there be a surplus of grain in the land,
    rustling on the mountain heights.

    May his fruit trees blossom like Lebanon,
    flourishing like the grass on the ground.

---

a The river referred to is the Euphrates.
b The location of Tarshish is uncertain, but most scholars would locate it in
  the western Mediterranean, in Spain or Sardinia perhaps.
c A kingdom in southwestern Arabia.

17 May his dynasty live to eternity!
   May they bear children until the sun fades away.

   May his dynasty be blessed through him;
   may all nations be made happy by him.

18 Praise the God Yahweh, the God of Israel,
   the only One who works marvels.

19 Praise his name and his glory forever.
   May all the earth be filled with his glory.

   Amen! Amen!

   (The prayers of David, son of Jesse,
   are at an end.)

Psalm 73 (72)

A psalm of innocence. Though commentators have generally believed this poem to be a product of the wisdom schools, a close examination of its contents reveals that the psalm is a declaration of the psalmist's innocence, closely related to other poems of this nature such as Psalms 16 and 17. In verses 1 and 2 the poet states the dilemma that he faced: God's role vis-à-vis the psalmist's difficulty. Verses 3 to 12 develop the causes of his temptation: the prosperity of the wicked seems to derive directly from their defiance and arrogance toward God. The poet describes his crisis in verses 13 to 15. But then he discovers the real future of the wicked in verses 16-20. The psalmist realizes that God himself is his reward (verses 21 to 26). Finally the psalmist states the conclusion to the dilemma he began the psalm with (verses 27 and 28). The psalmist has thus effectively declared that he never gave in to the temptation to follow the logic of godless men, and also states his confidence in the divine reward he is sure of.

1 *A psalm of Asaph.*

Despite everything, God is goodness itself for the upright;
that is what God is for the single-hearted.

2 Yet my feet nearly slipped,
and my legs had all but collapsed.

3 For I was envious of those who boast,
and looked with longing at the prosperity of evil men.

4 Truly they do not have hardships;
their bodies are strong and healthy.

5 The hard lot of ordinary mortals is not for them;
nor are they struck by torments like other people.

6 That is why arrogance is their necklace,
and the brazen finery of violence is their garment.

7 Their eyes are crafty and eager;
the schemes of their hearts exceed all bounds.

8   They scoff as they whisper their malice;
    arrogantly they discuss oppression.

9   With their mouths they defy heaven
    and with their tongues they challenge even the
        world below.

10   They quickly gorge themselves with everything
    and even drink up all the waters of the sea.

11   Then they declare: "Just where is God's
        providence?"
    "Does the Most High have knowledge?"

12   That is how the evil men are:
    they ignore the Eternal One
    and yet increase their wealth.

13   So it was in vain I kept my heart pure
    and washed my hands in innocence!

14   So it was in vain that I was struck with torments
        all day long.
    and punished anew morning after morning.

15   If I were to declare "I too will calculate like
        that,"
    I would have destroyed the assembly of your sons.

16   I pondered on how to understand this
    but it was too difficult for me,

17   until I went into the sanctuary of God
    and reflected on what their final goal would be.

18   Despite everything you will certainly transplant
        them into the Land of Perdition,
    make them fall into Desolation.

19   Suddenly they will be in Devastation;
    their course will end and they will disappear in
        that Land of Terrors.

20 Like a dream one disregards upon waking, Lord,
    you will have little regard for them
    in the City of Shadows.

21 But when my mind had gone stagnant
    and my emotions had hardened,

22 I was ignorant and did not understand;
    I was like a brainless beast before you.

23 Yet I will always be with you.
    Take me by the right hand, (24) lead me into
            your council,
    and take me up with glory.

25 What do I need in heaven?
    If I am with you, I delight in nothing on earth.

26 Though my flesh and my heart waste away,
    God is the Mountain of my heart
    and my portion is the Eternal One.

27 As for those who go far away from you, they will
            go to ruin;
    you will destroy everyone who is unfaithful to
            you.

28 For me, nearness to God is the good I possess;
    I have made Yahweh my Sovereign Lord and my
            refuge
    while I go on proclaiming what you have done.

Psalm 74 (73)

A national lament. This poem bewails bitterly the invasion of the sacred land by destructive enemies. Many scholars have attempted to identify the scenes of destruction portrayed in the psalms with the actual destruction of Jerusalem by the Babylonians in 587 B.C. Their efforts, however, have not proved entirely fruitful. For one thing, the mention of "Zion" in verse 2 may be the addition of a later hand. It is even conceivable that the psalm originated in the northern kingdom. In any case, the poem appeals to God who has seemingly abandoned his people and describes the wreckage that the invaders have brought about (verses 1-12). Verses 13-17 recall that Yahweh won the greatest of all victories at the time of his defeat of chaos and its monster-henchmen. The last portion of the poem (verses 18-23) appeals again to the pity of God, and beseeches him not to abandon his helpless people.

1   *A maskil of Asaph.*

    Why, O God, are you always angry?
    Why does your wrath smolder against the sheep
        you tend?

2   Remember the flock you acquired so long ago.
    Use your staff to redeem Mount Zion,
    that estate of yours on which you reside.

3   Raise your people up from utter ruin.
    The foe has wrecked everything in the sanctuary.

4   Your enemies have yelled even in your assembly!
    They planted their standards by the hundreds!

5   They set fire to the entrance
    and hacked at the paneling with axes.

6   They chopped all its doors down,
    battering with hatchets and sledge-hammers.

7   They consigned your sanctuary to the flames,
    desecrated the dwelling-place of your name.

8 In their hearts they said:
"Let all their descendants be burned—
all the congregations of God in the land!"

9 We see no portents now.
There are no more prophets.

10 Who among us, O God, even knows
how long the enemy will disgrace you?
How long, O Conqueror, will the foe deride you?

11 Why do you draw your left hand back
and keep your right hand close to you?

12 O God, destroy the kings from the East,
win victories here at the center of the world.

13 You are the one who split the sea by your might.
You are the one who smashed the heads of
Tannin,
the treacherous monster of the waters;

you are the one who crushed the heads of
Leviathan;
14 you gave him as food to the desert tribes.

15 You are the one who unleashed the springs and
rivers,
who turned the primeval floods into dry land.

16 To you belongs the day;
to you belongs the night as well.

17 You are the one who fixed the sun and the moon
at their stations.
You are the one who determined
all the climates of the earth;
it was you also who patterned summer and winter,

18 Remember this: an enemy has been taunting you,
Yahweh!
A foolish people has been scorning your name.

19 Do not give the life of your dove over to wild
     beasts;
  do not, forget the life of your afflicted people,
     O Conqueror.

20 Consider the state of your covenant:
  the city is full of darkness,
  the countryside, full of idolatry.

21 Do not let the disheartened sit ashamed;
  let the needy and the poor praise your name.

22 Arise, O God, and champion your cause;
  remember the abuse which fools heap on you all
     the day.

23 Do not forget the uproar that your adversaries
     make,
  nor the tumult that is constantly going up
  from those who attack you.

Psalm 75 (74)

It is not easy to classify this psalm in the usual categories. It may have been used in the liturgy as a little hymn of confidence in the victory of Yahweh over evil. It begins and ends with verses (2, 10) that suggest triumphant thanksgiving. Sandwiched between these verses is an oracle, a divine promise, that the Lord will indeed put an end to the blasphemies of his enemies, who appear to be idolatrous men. These foes of the Lord are boasters, confident of their own power. They put no faith in the Lord's judgment, in which he will redress wrongs and give his people what they hope for. The psalmist declares the Lord's universal dominion (verses 7-8) and warns that he will punish his enemies in a frightful manner (verse 9). The final verse reiterates the Lord's determination to carry out his threat. Although the language is archaic, it is impossible to date this psalm though it probably was used before the exile.

1   *For the director: "Do not destroy . . . "*
    A psalm of Asaph: a song.

2   We thank you, O God.
    We give you praise, because you are always near.
    We recount the wonders you have done.

3   "I shall convoke the assembly
    and I shall judge with fairness.

4   Though the earth may quake and all its
        inhabitants,
    it is I who steady its foundations.

5   I make this declaration: 'Boasters, do not boast;
    wicked men, do not toss your horns.' "[a]

6   Do not toss your horns against the Exalted One,
    nor charge against the Ancient Mountain.'

---

a The action of an angry bull: the metaphor suggests confidence in one's own power.

7 He is the Victor from east to west,
   Victor from the desert in the south
   to the mountains in the north.

8 It is God who is Judge:
   he is the one who humiliates
   and he is the one who exalts.

9 In the hand of Yahweh
   there is a cup, a bowl full of wine;[b]
   he will draw it and pour from it.

   Even its dregs will be drained;
   the wicked of the earth will drink all of it."

10 But I will praise the Eternal One;
   I will sing hymns to the God of Jacob.

11 And I shall break off the horns of the wicked
   but the horns of the Just One will be raised high.

[b] The cup of the Lord's wrath was an image of God's anger which his enemies would have to "drink." It was the cup from which Jesus asked to be spared (cf. Mark 14:36).

Psalm 76 (75)

A hymn of the divine victory. This psalm celebrates the divine protection of God's people. It commemorates a great divine triumph, but not necessarily any particular historical event. The ultimate foes may be evil forces who are spoken of in terms of actual historical enemies who are driven away from the people and the land of God. The particular feature of this psalm is the description of God as a mighty lion (cf. verses 3, 6, 7) whose very roar terrifies his foes.

1   *For the director: for strings. A psalm of Asaph; a song.*

2   God has manifested himself in Judah;
    his name has become famous in Israel.

3   His lair was in Salem,[a]
    his den on Zion.

4   There with his thunderbolts he smashed the bow,
    the shield and sword and stockpile of arms.

5   What awe you inspired,
    O God of Brilliant Light!

6   They would have despoiled the mountains of the
        Lion—
    those stouthearted men—

    but they slept their last sleep and were found no
        more.
    Those trained men of valor met their end.

7   God of Jacob, when you roared,
    chariots and horses froze in terror.

8   How awesome you are!
    Who can stand up to your fury,
    to your age-old wrath?

---

a Salem: an archaic name for Jerusalem.

9   You will thunder your decision from heaven;
     earth will shudder and fall silent

10   when God arises for the judgment
     to save all the lowly of the earth.

11   Filled with joy they will praise you;
     the survivors will be overjoyed
     and will feast in your honor.[b]

12   Make your promises and fulfill them
     to Yahweh, your God;
     let all around bring offerings to him.

     Let them bring offerings
13   to the Watcher who proves the spirit of princes.
     He is frightful to the kings of the earth.

[b] The Hebrew of this verse is very uncertain. The present translation is based on that of Moses Buttenwieser (*The Psalms*, N.Y., 1969, p. 110).

Psalm 77 (76)

Though the speaker in this psalm seems to be an individual, he is praying for the restoration of the fortunes of the whole people. Thus Psalm 77 is a lament of the nation, probably to be recited by a leader or king. The psalmist begins with a lengthy description of the situation (verses 2-11): the state of the country is lamentable. God seems no longer to listen to prayer. The second part of the psalm (verses 12-16) recalls the wonders of creation and concludes with a prayer for deliverance. Verses 17-20, which in the Hebrew have a rhythm distinct from the earlier part of the poem, may be a later addition. Using different phrases the creation battle of Yahweh is again recalled, and verse 21 adds a final petition for divine help. This psalm seems to have had a northern Israelite origin.

1   *For the director: according to Jeduthun. A psalm of Asaph.*

2   With a desperate cry I call, O God of gods;
    listen at once to my cry, O God of gods.

3   By day I implore my God
    and I look for my Sovereign Lord.
    In the night I reach out my hand without tiring.
    My soul refuses to be comforted.

4   I remember God, but then I moan;
    I meditate, but then my spirit grows weary.

5   My eyes have grown used to wakefulness;
    I pace back and forth and do not lie down.

6   I ponder on the days of old,[a]
    and call to mind the years of long ago.

7   In the night I strum my lyre.
    I reflect in my heart
    and my spirit goes deep into a question:

---

a   The "days of old" are the times when God won his victories, over chaos, at the time of creation.

8   "Will the Sovereign Lord be angry forever?
Will he never show favor again?

9   Has his unfailing love come to an end?
Has his oracle to all generations become silent?

10   Has the source of God's compassion now dried
up?
Has anger chilled his loving heart?"

11   I thought: The problem is this:
The right hand of the Most High has grown
feeble!

12   I will call to mind your superb works;
yes, I will recall your marvels from of old.

13   I will meditate on all your actions,
and I will ponder on your works.

14   Your dominion, O God, extends
over the assembly of the holy ones.
What god is as great as you, O God?

15   You are the God who performs your miraculous
deeds,
making your power known among the nations.

16   Redeem your people with you own arm—
the sons of Jacob and Joseph.

17   The waters saw you, O God;
the sea's waters saw you and began to churn.
The very abyss shook in terror.

18   Water burst from the clouds,
the sky re-echoed with your thunder-voice,
and your arrows of lightning flashed back and
forth.

19   The clap of your thunder was hurled
across the vault of the sky;
the flashes of your lightning illumined all the land,
and the world below shuddered and shook.

20 Your path led across the sea,
    your steps took you through the waters of the
        deep;
    your tracks could not be seen.

21 Lead your people like a flock again
    by the hand of a Moses and an Aaron.

Psalm 78 (77)

Psalm 78 was composed in the southern kingdom of Judah in a time when the Jerusalem temple still stood and the dynasty of King David was still on the throne. The opening verses (1-8) suggest that the psalmist's purpose was didactic: the lengthy recital that follows should serve as a warning about continued fidelity to God. Then follows an extended description of the exodus, the occupation of the promised land, and the ultimate rejection of the northern tribes (verses 9-67), in which the tribe of Ephraim comes in for very unfavorable criticism. Finally (verses 68-72) the psalmist extols the Lord's selection of David, Judah, and Mount Zion. How this psalm was used in ancient Israel must remain an open question. But it retains today its stern admonition that God will reject those who spurn his advances.

1 *A maskil of Asaph.*

My people, pay attention to my instruction;
turn your ear to the words I am going to speak.

2 I will begin my discourse with a parable;
I will disclose the enigma of the distant past—

3 things we have heard and known,
things our fathers have recounted to us.

4 We will not conceal them from their
    grandchildren;
we will repeat them for the next generation:
the glorious deeds of Yahweh, and his conquest,
and the miracles that he performed.

5 He issued a decree in Jacob;
in Israel he established a law
that what he commanded our fathers,
they should make known to their sons;

6 that the next generation, the children yet to be
    born,
would know and in turn tell their own children,

7 so they might place their confidence in God
   and not forget the divine works
   but keep his commandments,

8 instead of becoming like their ancestors—
   a rebellious and unruly generation,

   a generation whose hearts were not firm in
        their purpose,
   whose spirits were unfaithful to God.

9 The sons of Ephraim were his bowmen,
   his unreliable archers:
   they turned tail on the day of battle.

10 They did not keep the covenant with God,
   but refused to walk according to his instructions.

11 They forgot his deeds
   and the miracles he had let them see.

12 In the presence of their fathers he had done
        wonders
   in the land of Egypt, on the plain of Zoan.

13 He split the sea to let them pass through,
   making the water stand as solid as a dike.

14 By day he guided them with a cloud
   and all night long by the light of a fire.

15 He split the rocks in the desert
   and watered even that vast and sandy waste.

16 He made streams jet from the rock
   and caused them to cascade like rivers.

17 But they continued to sin against him,
   rebelling against the Most High there in the
        wasteland.

18 They put God on trial in their hearts
   by asking for food to stuff themselves.

19 They complained about God,
saying: "Can God set a table in the wilderness?

20 Yes, he struck a rock and water spurted out
and gullies overflowed—
but can he supply bread as well?
Can he provide his people with meat?"

21 Now, when Yahweh heard this
there was no limit to his anger;
his fire raged against Jacob
and his wrath blazed up against Israel.

22 But they put no faith in God,
no trust in his saving power.

23 Yet he commanded the clouds above
and opened the portals of heaven:

24 he rained manna down on them for food—
he gave them the grain of heaven.

25 Everyone ate bread of the angels—
the provisions he had sent them in abundance.

26 He unleased the east wind from heaven
and led the south wind out of his fortress;

27 he rained meat on them like dust
and flying birds like the sands of the seashore.

28 He made them fall right into their camp—
and around their dwellings.

29 So they ate and were well satisfied:
he had brought them what they craved.

30 But they did not restrain their greed
even while the food was still in their mouths.

31 So, the anger of God blazed up against them.
He slew the healthiest among them,
striking down the finest of Israel's youth.

32 In spite of this they went on sinning—
they put no faith in his wonders.

33 He made their days vanish more swiftly than mist,
their years more quickly than a fleeting phantom.

34 When he began to destroy them,
they would seek him;
then they would repent and long for God.

35 They remembered that God was their Mountain,
and that God, the Most High, was their
Redeemer.

36 But they deceived him with their mouths,
lying to him with their tongues.

37 Their hearts were not solidly fixed on him,
and they were unfaithful to the covenant with
him.

38 But he is the Compassionate One;
he forgave their guilt and did not destroy them.

Instead, he kept on turning back his anger
and would stoke up none of his rage.

39 And he remembered that they were only flesh—
a breeze that blows by, and does not come back.

40 How often they revolted against him in the
wilderness,
and caused him suffering in the desert!

41 Over and over they put God on trial
and made the Holy One of Israel sad.

42 They did not remember his power
nor the day he had ransomed them from the
enemy,

43 when he had performed his wonders in Egypt
and his marvels on the Plain of Zoan.

44 He turned their rivers into blood
so they could not drink from their streams.

45 He sent flies to devour them
and frogs to destroy them.

46 He consigned their crops to the grasshopper,
their hard-won fruits to the locust.

47 He killed their vines with hail
and their berries with frost.

48 He condemned their cattle to the hail,
their flocks to the thunderbolts.

49 He loosed his blazing anger among them—
rage and fury and destruction,
an escort of harmful angels (50) to level a path
before him.

He did not spare them from death
but delivered their lives to the plague.

51 He struck down all the first-born in Egypt—
the first fruits of their vigor born in the tents of
Ham.

52 Then he led his people out like sheep,
guiding them like a flock through the wilderness.

53 Confident and unhurried he escorted them
while the sea buried their enemies.

54 He brought them to his holy uplands—
the mountains his right hand had acquired.

55 He drove the nations before them
and let their inheritance fall to them by lot;
he let the tribes of Israel dwell in their tents.

56 But they put God on trial and revolted against
him;
they did not pay attention to the Most High
and his decrees.

57 They turned away, and played him false
          like their fathers,
     useless like a bow that is slack.

58 They annoyed him with their high-places
     and made him jealous with their idols.

59 God heard of it
     and there was no limit to his anger,
     and he rejected Israel completely.

60 He departed from his residence at Shiloh,
     the tent he had pitched among men.

61 He abandoned his fortress, his glorious ark,
     into the hands of his enemies, to be captured.

62 He delivered his people to the sword
     and there was no limit to his anger against
          his patrimony.

63 Fire devoured their young men,
     so their maidens were not praised in wedding
          songs.

64 Their priests fell by the sword
     and their widows sang no laments.

65 Then the Lord awoke as though from sleep,
     like a warrior who had rested after his wine.

66 He struck his enemies from behind
     and heaped everlasting shame upon them.

67 He rejected the tents of Joseph,
     and did not choose the tribe of Ephraim.

68 Instead, he chose the tribe of Judah,
     and Mount Zion, which he loved.

69 There he built his sanctuary
     to be like the heights of heaven,
     like the earth that he had founded from eternity.

70 And he chose David, his servant,
   lifting him out of the sheepfolds.

71 From chasing ewes he brought him
   to shepherd Jacob, his people,
   and Israel, his patrimony.

72 He shepherded them with single heart
   and led them with his skillful hands.

Psalm 79 (78)

A national lament. This psalm may have been composed after one of the defeats that Jerusalem suffered in the course of its history. It was probably used to complain to God of the wretched condition in which the southern kingdom often found itself. 1 Maccabees 7:17 makes use of verses 2-3 of this psalm on just such an occasion, and doubtless the psalm was of venerable age even at that time.

1 *A psalm of Asaph.*

O God, the nations have entered your estate.
They have defiled your holy temple
and made Jerusalem a mound of ruins.

2 They have left the corpses of your servants
as carrion for the birds of the air—
the flesh of those devoted to you
as food for the beasts of the earth.

3 They have shed blood like water
and there was not one person around Jerusalem
to bury the dead.

4 We have become a thing for our neighbors to
abuse,
something to make fun of, something to laugh at.

5 How long, O Yahweh?
Will you stay angry with us forever?
How long will your jealousy burn like fire?

6 Pour out your rage on the nations
that do not recognize you,
and upon the kingdoms
that do not call on your name.

7 They have devoured Jacob
and devastated his quiet home.

8 Do not hold our ancestors' guilt against us:
come swiftly to meet us with your tender mercy,
because we have come a long way down.

9 Help us, God of our salvation!
Rescue us for the glory of your name.

For the sake of that name
forgive us our sins:

10 otherwise the nations will say:
"Where is their God?"

Let us see your name recognized among the
nations;
avenge your servants' blood which was shed.

11 Let the sighing of the prisoners
enter into your presence;
with your mighty arm
reprieve those condemned to die.

12 And pay back seven times over
into the bosom of our neighbors
the abuse they have heaped upon you, O
Sovereign Lord.

13 But we will thank you forever—
we, your people and the flock that you shepherd.
From generation to generation
we will recount your praise.

Psalm 80 (79)

A national lament. The northern kingdom of Israel was the setting in which Psalm 80 was used. Like Psalm 44, the present poem complains of the nation's abandonment despite its fidelity to the covenant. Verses 2-8 depict the present situation of disaster, perhaps giving a description of the weakness of the kingdom in the decades before the fall of Samaria in 721 B.C. Verses 9-14 contrast the helplessness of Israel with its prosperity in earlier times. Verses 15-20 constitute a plea for help for both king and people.

1 *For the director: according to "Lilies". A solemn commandment: a psalm of Asaph.*

2 Listen now, O Shepherd of Israel:
guide Joseph like a flock!
You, whose throne is the cherubim, appear in
light

3 before Ephraim, Benjamin and Manasseh.
Awaken your power and come to our rescue.

4 O God, come back to us:
look on us kindly so we may be saved.

5 O Yahweh, God of power and might,
how long will you go on fuming
while your people pray?

6 You have fed us tears for food
and given us tears by the bowlful to drink.

7 You have made us
the prize of our neighbors' wrangling:
our enemies have made us
the target of their scorn.

8 O God of power and might, come back to us:
look on us kindly so we may be saved.

9 You brought a grapevine from Egypt:
you drove out the nations and planted it;

10   you cleared a space for it
     and made it take root and fill the land.

11   Mountains were covered by its shade—
     the tallest cedars, by its branches.

12   It put vines out all the way to the sea—
     its tendrils, as far as the River.[a]

13   Why have you wrecked its hedge
     so everyone who passes by can pick its fruit?

14   Wild pigs from the forest have chewed it up,
     and creatures of the field have fed on it.

15   Now then, God of power and might,
     turn toward us;
     look down from heaven—look at this
     and inspect this grapevine.

16   Take care of what your own hand has planted,
     your son,[b] whom you made strong for yourself.

17   Those who burned it in a scorching fire—
     may they perish at your furious rebuke.

18   Let your hand rest on the man at your right, [c]
     upon that son of man
     whom you made strong for yourself.

19   We have never turned away from you;
     bring us back to life
     so we may call on your Name.

20   Yahweh, God of power and might,
     come back to us:
     look on us kindly so we may be saved.

---

a The Euphrates River is meant—this stream was the northernmost boundary of Israelite influence in antiquity.
b "Son": the king of Israel.
c "Man at your right": still another term for the king of Israel.

Psalm 81 (80)

This psalm is generally classified as a prophetic liturgy. It was used probably for the feast of tabernacles in the autumn. It falls readily into two parts. Verses 2-5 sound like the beginning of a hymn. Verses 6-15 seem to be the words of a prophet or other leader who presents a message of warning from Yahweh, harking back to the exodus and threatening a sinister fate if Israel does not listen to the voice of the Lord now. Verses 16-17 conclude the poem on a positive note of hope. The psalm originated in the northern kingdom.

1   *For the director: on the gittith. A psalm of Asaph.*

2   Shout with joy to God, our Fortress;
     shout in triumph to the God of Jacob.

3   Strike up a song, sound the tambourine,
     the pleasing lyre and the harp.

4   Blow the trumpet at the new moon,
     at the full moon, the solemn day of our feast.

5   This is a law, O Israel,
     a ruling from the God of Jacob.

6   He made it a solemn commandment for Joseph
     as he was departing from the land of Egypt.

     "I listened to the voice
     of one I had not yet recognized.

7   I removed the burden from his shoulder,
     and liberated his hands from the basket.

8   You called from distress and I rescued you;
     from the hidden home of the thunder I answered
       you,
     though you had provoked me at the waters of
       Meribah.

9   O my people,
     listen while I give testimony against you;
     O Israel, if only you would listen to me.

10 There is not to be a foreign god among you,
    and you are not to bow down before an alien god.

11 I myself am Yahweh, your God,
    who brought you up from the land of Egypt.
    Moreover, I filled your gaping mouth.

12 But my people did not listen to my voice,
    and Israel had no interest in me.

13 I dismissed them to the obstinacy of their hearts,
    and they walked according to their own plans.

14 If only my people would listen to me!
    If only Israel would walk in my ways,

15 I would quickly subdue their foes,
    and turn my hand against their adversaries!

16 Yahweh's enemies would cringe before him,
    and their submission would be perpetual.

17 He would feed Israel with the richest wheat,
    and regale them with the choicest honey."

Psalm 82 (81)

A prophetic liturgy in which a prophet gives a poetic insight
into a heavenly decision. The scene described in the psalm is
somewhat jarring to the contemporary Christian outlook: God
is described as he presides over a pantheon of lesser gods,
somewhat as El, the chief Canaanite deity, kept order among
his inferiors. These deities had been charged with maintaining
right order in the world, but they have failed miserably in that
task. It is for this that they are indicted by God in verses 1-5.
Verses 6-7 present the judgment of these wicked incompetents:
they are to lose their immortality, a divine prerogative, and die
like men. Verse 8 is a final appeal to God to see to the
performing of justice himself.

The Christian realizes that he has a poem before him and
that the images of this psalm, though foreign to him, contain a
message that is still valid today: God is above all powers,
human or otherwise. His providence is worthy of trust and all
his children should look for it and pray for it.

1   *A psalm of Asaph.*

    God presides over the divine assembly
    and among the gods he passes judgment:

2   "How long will you hand down unfair decisions—
    how long will you be partial to the wicked?

3   Defend the helpless and the fatherless!
    Do justice for the needy and the destitute!

4   Deliver the helpless and the poor!
    Rescue them from the grasp of the wicked!"

5   They know nothing and understand nothing;
    they wander around in the darkness
    while all the foundations of the world are
        tottering.

6   "You are gods," I had declared,
    "all of you are sons of the Most High! "

7   But no—you are going to die like ordinary men;
    like mere functionaries you are going to fall.

8   Stand up, O God,
    and pass judgment over all the earth:
    govern all the nations yourself.

Psalm 83 (82)

While no exact date can be determined for this national lament, it must have originated sometime before the fall of Assyria (mentioned in verse 9) in 612 B.C. Since the psalm may well come from the northern kingdom of Israel its composition may even antedate the fall of that kingdom in 721 B.C. The psalm describes a coalition of the foes of Israel (verses 3-9) most of which were relatively powerless states, but their military might had been reinforced by Assyria, the imperialist terror of the ancient Near East. Verses 10-19 call upon God to defeat and destroy these enemies as he obliterated the boastful assailants of Israel in times long past.

1 *A psalm; a song of Asaph.*

2 O God, do not be speechless and reserved;
   do not be silent and passive, O God.

3 See how your foes are making loud noises;
   your enemies are holding their heads high.

4 They are laying secret, cunning plans against
        your people,
   plotting together against those you cherish.

5 They have made this decision:
   "Come, let us abolish them as a people," and
   "Let the name 'Israel' be no longer remembered."

6 Yes, they are plotting and are in agreement,
   they are signing a treaty against you—

7 the tents of Edom and the Ishmaelites,
   those of Moab and the Hagarites,[a]

---

a Edom, Ishmael, Moab, Hagar: desert tribes, more or less organized, which harassed Israel from time to time, especially when she had foes elsewhere to worry about.

[185]

8   Byblos[b] as well as Amalek,[c]
    Philistia[d] and the citizens of Tyre,[e]

9   Even Assyria has joined with them;
    they have become the mighty arm
    of the children of Lot.

10 Deal with them as you did with Midian,[f]
    as with Sisera and Jabin at Kishon Creek.[g]

11 Let them be obliterated from the face of the
        earth;
    let them serve to fertilize the ground.

12 Make their nobles like Oreb and Zeeb,
    all their chiefs like Zebah and Zalmunna, (13) who
        said:
    "Let us take the finest meadows for ourselves."

14 My God, make them like tumbleweeds,
    like straw in the wind.

15 As fire burns a forest,
    as flame sets mountains ablaze,

16 pursue them with your storm,
    torment them with your hurricane.

17 Cover their faces with chagrin,
    and seek vengeance for your name, O Yahweh.

18 May they live in endless humiliation and
        harassment,
    to be disgraced and finally to perish.

---

[b] Byblos: a Phoenician city on the Syrian coast, in modern Lebanon.
[c] Amalek: descendants of Esau, living around the borders of Israel, and raiding
    when they could.
[d] Gentile enemies located southwest of Israel.
[e] A Phoenician city on the coast.
[f] Midian: a tribe of marauding Bedouin in the region of the Gulf of Akabah.
[g] Sisera and Jabin: cf. Judges 4. Jabin was king of Hazor in the time of the
    Judges, and Sisera was his young general, who provoked the Israelites, but
    was finally defeated and died a disgraceful death.

19   Let them know that your name is Yahweh
     and that you alone are the Most High
     over all the earth.

Psalm 84 (83)

A psalm whose classification has long eluded the best efforts of scholars. It may be a pilgrimage song, but there are elements in this poem of so many different types that none of them are determinative for the whole psalm. Verses 2-6 speak of the longing of the poet for Yahweh. Verses 7-8 speak of a pilgrimage, though the meaning of the Hebrew is far from certain; the location and even the existence of the "Balsam Valley" are in question. Verses 9-10 appear to be a prayer for the king. Verses 11-13 are expressions of trust in Yahweh as the source of life, mercy, and the all-important gift of rain, as over against idols who are the lords only of the nether-world (verse 11).

1　*For the director: on the gittith.*
　A psalm of the sons of Korah.

2　How lovely is the place where you dwell,
　O Yahweh of power and might!

3　My soul craves—yes, it is even consumed
　for the court of Yahweh;
　my heart and my flesh cry out:
　O God, O living God!

4　Even the sparrow finds her home
　and the swallow a nest for herself;
　there she puts her young beside your altars,
　O Yahweh of power and might,
　my king, my God.

5　How blest are they who dwell in your house
　where they sing your unceasing praises.

6　How blest the man whose strength is in you,
　your praises in his heart.

7　As they go through the Balsam Valley,
　they make it a place of springs,
　clothed in blessings by the early rains.

8　They proceed from village to village
　to see the God of gods in Zion.

9 O Yahweh, God of power and might,
   hear my prayer:
   listen closely, O God of Jacob.

10 O God, our suzerain,
   look upon the face of the one you have anointed.

11 Far better is one day in your court
   than a thousand in the grave!
   Far better to dwell
   at the threshold of the house of my God,
   than to abide in the tents of Death!

12 Sun and suzerain is Yahweh God
   who gives kindness and honor.
   Yahweh will not withhold his beneficial rain
   from those who walk virtuously.

13 Yahweh of power and might,
   how blest is the man who puts his trust in you!

Psalm 85 (84)

A prayer for rain. This poem was used in the liturgy for the autumn feast. It falls into two parts. Verses 2-8 pray that the drought of summer may soon end. The sins of the people have driven God from the land, but the psalmist is confident of forgiveness and the return of a God no longer angry. Verses 9-14 are a sort of oracle in which the leader of the community, perhaps a prophet, speaks of God's plan for the coming year: prosperity for a people faithful to the Lord. His generosity will reach down to meet the loyalty of his people which extends its hands to him. The heaven-sent rain is an image of the mercy of God.

1   *For the director: a psalm of the sons of Korah.*

2   Show favor to your land, O Yahweh:
    give a good harvest time [a] to Jacob again.

3   Remove the guilt of your people
    and cover all their sins.

4   Withdraw all your anger;
    take away the fury of your wrath.

5   Come back to us, O God of our prosperity.
    Let your irritation with us disappear.

6   Will you be angry with us forever?
    Will you prolong your wrath
    from one generation to the next?

7   You are the Conqueror:
    restore life to us again
    and you will make your people glad.

8   Show us your unfailing love, O Yahweh,
    and give us your prosperity.

---

[a] "Good harvest time": the Hebrew suggests the notion here of the whole growing cycle.

9 Let me proclaim
what God himself has revealed:
Yahweh has announced prosperity
for those devoted to him
and for those who have confidence in him again.

10 Truly, his prosperity is near
to those who reverence him.
His glory will dwell in our land again.

11 The kindness of God
and the loyalty of man will meet;
his justice and their prosperity will embrace.

12 Loyalty will sprout up from the earth
and justice will lean down from heaven.

13 Yahweh will bestow his generous rain
with a clap of thunder
and our land will yield its harvest.

14 Lush abundance will march ahead of him
and springtime beauty will follow in his footsteps.

Psalm 86 (85)

Psalm 86 is a royal lament, the prayer of a king beseeching God for rescue from calamity. The phraseology of the poem is traditional and there is not a great deal of originality in the composition. Still the whole has a note of pathos and urgency about it that makes it a fitting prayer in time of duress and depression.

1 *A prayer of David.*

    Turn your ear toward me, Yahweh, and answer
        me,
    because I am afflicted and poor.

2 Protect my life,
    because I am devoted to you.

    Save your own servant, my God,
    because I put my trust in you.

3 Have pity, O Sovereign Lord,
    because I call to you all the day.

4 Gladden the soul of your servant
    because for you, O Sovereign Lord,
    I am waiting in suspense.

5 You are good and forgiving, O Sovereign Lord,
    rich in unfailing love
    toward all who call upon you.

6 Yahweh, listen to my prayer;
    be attentive when I cry out for mercy.

7 On the day that I am besieged, I call you:
    if only you would answer me!

8 Among the gods, there is not one like you,
    nor anything like your works, O Sovereign Lord.

9 If you take action all nations will come
    and bow down before you, O Sovereign Lord,
    and they will glorify your name.

10 How great you are, O Worker of wonders—
you alone, O God.

11 Yahweh, teach me your way,
and I will walk faithful to you alone.
Teach my heart to reverence your name.

12 I will thank you, Yahweh, my God,
with all my heart;
I will glorify your name, O Everlasting One.

13 Because your unfailing love is great, O Most High,
you will rescue my soul from the depths of Sheol.

14 O God, arrogant men have risen up against me,
and the council of foreign savages
is seeking my life.
They do not acknowledge you as their leader.

15 But, O Sovereign Lord, you are God,
the Compassionate and the Merciful,
slow to anger
but rich in unfailing love and faithfulness.

16 Turn to me and have pity on me.
Give conquest to your servant;
give victory to your faithful son.

17 Perform for me some token act of your kindness,
so my enemies may see it and be humiliated.
If only you would help me
and console me yourself, O Yahweh!

Psalm 87 (86)

A song of Zion, in which the holy city is praised as the chosen dwelling of God and a prophecy of its future glory is pronounced. Possibly this poem was composed around the time of the exile when the fortunes of Jerusalem were at a low ebb. But the psalmist retains his faith that Zion was founded by Yahweh and that she is still his favorite dwelling (verses 1-2). Moreover, the psalmist predicts that the time will come when foreigners, even the present enemies of Yahweh, will rejoice to claim citizenship in the sacred city and that the Lord will consider these enemies of former times to be natives of his chosen race (verses 3-7).

1   *A psalm; a song of the sons of Korah.*

    O city, founded by Yahweh
    on the holy mountains!

2   He loves you, O gates of Zion,
    more than all the splendid shrines of Jacob.

3   In you, O city of God, he says:

4   "I shall list Egyptian Rahab[a] and Babylon too,
    among those who recognize me,

    Philistia and Tyre as well,
    and even Ethiopia—
    they are native-born citizens."

5   And of Zion it will be said:
    "Each and every man was born in her,"
    and "The Most High will make her secure."

6   In the registry of the peoples, Yahweh will write:
    "They are native-born citizens."

7   And as they sing and dance they will say:
    "All my origins are in you!"

---

a Rahab: a mythological sea-monster whose name means "stormy one" or "arrogant one". The name stands for powers that rebel against Yahweh and was an epithet for Egypt.

Psalm 88 (87)

An individual lament. But this psalm is a particularly striking lament, for it ends on a note that is most melancholy, almost despairing. There is no promise of praise here, no confidence that the psalmist will find quick aid from Yahweh. Perhaps the most that can be said is that the psalmist *is* praying. Beginning with a request to be heard (verses 2-3), the poet states his misery (verses 4-10). Though this is described with much feeling (the psalmist cries out from the world of the dead) it cannot be stated exactly what his affliction was. Verses 11-13 remind Yahweh of the inability of those in Sheol to join in the liturgical worship of his people, but the psalmist is still able to make his plea known (verses 14-15). The last part of the psalm (verses 16-19) gives an even more graphic description of the psalmist's wretchedness than was presented earlier.

1 *A song; a psalm of the sons of Korah. For the director: according to Mahalath Leannoth. A maskil of Heman, the native.*

2 Yahweh, my God, my deliverer!
   By day I call to you for help
   and by night I call out in your presence.

3 Let my prayer come before you;
   listen to my ringing cry

4 for my soul is filled with distress
   and my life has arrived at Sheol.

5 I am numbered
   among those who go down into the Pit
   and have become like a warrior
   who has no strength.

6 My mat is in the realm of Death
   like the men who have been slain.
   My couch is in the grave
   like those you remember no more,
   who are separated from your love.

[195]

7 You have plunged me into the deepest pit,
in the darkness, in the depths.

8 Your fury weighs heavy on me
and you oppress me with all the waves of your
wrath.

9 You have put my friends far away from me,
made me an object of loathing.
I am imprisoned and I cannot escape.

10 My eyes have grown dim from suffering.
Every day, I call out to you: "Yahweh!"
And I lift up my hands to you.

11 Would you work a miracle for the dead?
Will those quiet ones rise and sing your praises?

12 In the grave do they recount your loving-kindness,
or, in the Land of the Lost, your faithfulness?

13 Are your wonders even known
in that place of Darkness,
or your generosity in that Land of Oblivion?

14 But I am calling to you for help, O Yahweh.
May my prayer enter into your presence at dawn.

15 O Yahweh, why do you loathe my soul—
why do you turn your face away from me?

16 I am afflicted—I am expiring while I groan;
I have borne your terrors—I am passing away.

17 The breakers of your anger have crested over
me—
your horrors have utterly destroyed me.

18 They engulf me like flood-waters all the day long;
they encompass me and I am all alone.

19 You have put my dear ones and my friends
far away from me.
My one companion is Darkness.

Psalm 89 (88)

A royal psalm of the Davidic dynasty. This poem begins with a brief overture (verses 2-5) and then enters on a hymn of creation (verses 6-19). This creation motif suggests that the psalm was originally used at the autumnal festival when the kingship was renewed. Then the great messianic oracle of Yahweh to King David is recounted (verses 20-38). Verses 39-46 contrast the great hopes of the past with the current debacle which the kingdom is suffering. The calamities told of in these verses are probably not as late as the exile, but doubtless are the troubles regularly suffered by the Jerusalem kingdom throughout its history. Finally (verses 47-52) the king utters a prayer for the restoration of the original fortunes of King David and those that God had promised. Verse 53 is a doxology inserted by a later editor to mark the end of Book III of the psalter in the Hebrew text.

1 *A maskil of Ethan the native.*

2 Your unfailing love, O Yahweh,
   I will sing forever;
   age after age I will publish your faithfulness.

3 Yes, my declaration will be:
   "Eternal One, your unfailing love built the
        heavens;
   your faithfulness is established even more firmly."

4 "I have made a covenant with the one I chose;
   I have sworn:

   'O David my servant,
5 I shall set up your dynasty to last till eternity;
   I have built your throne to endure age after
        age.'"

6 In the heavens they praise your promise, Yahweh,
   and your faithfulness in the assembly of the holy
        ones.

7 Who in the skies is Yahweh's equal?
   who is like Yahweh among the sons of the gods?

[197]

8   God inspires more dread
    than the assembly of the holy ones:
    he is greater and more awe-inspiring
    than all those around him.

9   Yahweh, God of power and might, who is like
        you?
    Mighty Yahweh, your faithful are all around you.

10   You it was who suppressed the greed of the sea-
        god;
    when his waves were swelling,
    you it was who stopped them.

11   You it was who reduced Rahab[a] to carrion
    and with your powerful arm
    you sent your enemies flying.

12   To you belong the heavens, to you the earth
        besides;
    you laid the foundations of the world
    and all it contains.

13   You it was who created Zaphan and Amana,
    Tabor and Hermon[b] shout for joy at your name.

14   Yours is a powerful arm!
    Your left hand is triumphant,
    your right hand held high in victory!

15   Justice and right judgment
    are the foundations of your throne;
    unfailing love and faithfulness march before you.

---

[a] Rahab: a legendary monster of chaos which Yahweh defeated when he created the world and set all things in order.

[b] Zaphan, Amana, Tabor, Hermon: significant mountains in Galilee and Lebanon. Probably they once contained pagan shrines, and their action in this verse implies that their deities were quite subordinate to Yahweh.

16 How happy the people that experiences your
          radiance;
     they walk, O Yahweh, in the light of your face!

17 They rejoice in your name all the day;
     they are wild with joy because of your generosity.

18 Yes, you are the splendor of our triumph,
     and through your good pleasure you give us
          victory.

19 Yes, Yahweh is indeed our suzerain;
     the Holy One of Israel is our king.

20 Long, long ago you spoke in a vision,
     saying to one who was devoted to you:

     "I chose a youth rather than a warrior
     to make him king;
     I elevated a boy above a hero.

21 I found my servant, David,
     and I anointed him with my holy oil.

22 My hand will make him powerful—
     my arm will make him strong.

23 No enemy will stand up to him,
     no vicious foe conquer him.

24 I shall hammer his enemies before him
     and pummel those who hate him.

25 But with him will be my faithfulness and
          unfailing love
     and by my name he will be victorious.

26 I shall set his left hand on the Sea,
     and his right hand on the Euphrates River.

27 He will call out to me: 'You are my Father,
     my God, my Mountain, my Deliverer!'

28 And I, for my part, shall name him my first-born,
and highest among the kings of the earth.

29 To eternity I shall preserve my unfailing love
toward him
and my covenant will be inviolable.

30 I shall preserve his dynasty forever
and his throne will last like the days of heaven.

31 If his sons abandon my law,
and if they will not walk according to my
decisions,

32 if they break my statutes
and do not keep my commandments:

33 Then I shall punish their rebellions with a rod,
and their malice with lashes.

34 But I shall never withdraw my loyalty from him,
never be deceitful in my faithfulness.

35 I shall not violate my covenant,
never renounce what has passed my lips.

36 Once I swore by my own holiness—
never will I lie to David!—

37 his dynasty will last till eternity,
and his throne will be like the sun in my presence.

38 Like the moon will his descendants live on,
and his throne will be more permanent than the
sky."

39 But now you have become angry,
and rejected your anointed one;
your rage at him has no bounds.

40 You have canceled the covenant with your
servant;
you have broken his crown on the ground.

41 You have breached all his walls,
   made rubble of all his fortresses.

42 Every passer-by is looting him;
   his neighbors have taken to scoffing at him.

43 You have held up his enemies' hand in victory
   and gladdened all his foes.

44 In anger you have turned his blade back on him
   instead of supporting his sword.

45 You have made his reputation decline among his
      troops
   and toppled his throne to the ground.

46 You have curtailed the days of his vigor
   and shrouded his youth in sterility.

47 Yahweh, how long will you turn away?
   How long, O Conqueror,
   will your anger blaze like fire?

48 Remember my sorrow
   and the few days of my life.
   Did you create all men for nothing?

49 Is anyone living who will not see death?
   What man can rescue himself from the grip of
      Sheol?

50 Where, O Sovereign Lord,
   are those former acts of your unfailing love,
   the ones you promised David by your faithfulness?

51 Remember, O Sovereign Lord
   the abuse your servant suffers—

   I carry in my heart all the barbs of the peoples,
52 with which your foes abuse me, O Yahweh,
   at every single step that your anointed one takes.

53 Praise Yahweh forever!
   Amen! Amen!

Psalm 90 (89)

Basically, Psalm 90 is a national lament, but there are elements of wisdom teaching contained in it. The nation has been suffering some grave calamity, perhaps a drought of long duration. This prayer reminds God of his eternity and his power (verses 1-2) and then recalls the brevity of human life and the helplessness of men (verses 3-12). Verses 13-17 utter the requests that the psalmist wishes to send up to God: that he return to the land (his "absence" would account for the drought, if drought is the affliction the people are suffering), that he pour out his covenant love on his people again, restore their fortunes and bless their works.

1   *A prayer of Moses, the man of God.*

O Sovereign Lord you have been our support,
generation after generation.

2   Before ever the mountains came to birth,
before land and world were born,
from eternity past until eternity to come you are.

3   Do not change man back into dust—
do not say: "Return, sons of Adam,"

4   because a thousand years just passsed before your
eyes
like yesterday, like a night-watch.

5   If you overwhelm them while they sleep,
at dawn they will be like dry stubble.[a]

6   If it blossoms and is mowed in the morning,
by evening it will be withered and dry.

7   Truly, we are burnt up in your anger,
brought to ruin by your rage.

---

[a] The Hebrew of verse 5 has not fully disclosed its meaning to scholars.

8 You have set our iniquities before your very eyes;
the sins of our youth
are under the searching light of your face.

9 Yes, our days have all vanished in your fury;
our years are used up as quickly as a sigh.

10 A mere seventy years is this life of ours,
or eighty at the most.
Struggle and toil are nothing else than
     presumption;
pleasure races by, and then we too disappear.

11 Who can understand the violence of your anger?
Who can understand your rage
against those who fear you?

12 Teach us to calculate the number of our days,
so we may attain the very heart of wisdom.

13 Come back, O Yahweh—
how long before you come back?
Act with tenderness toward your servants.

14 Fill us at dawn with your unfailing love,
so we may shout for joy and be happy all our
     days.

15 Make us happy as many days as you let us be
     afflicted,
as many years as we have been suffering evil.

16 And let this accomplishment of yours
be evident to your servants,
your dominion apparent to their children.

17 May the gentleness of the Sovereign Lord, our
     God, be upon us;
may he favor the work of our hands for us,
and favor the work of our hands for himself.

Psalm 91 (90)

A royal psalm of trust. A court poet or prophet would have
recited this psalm to the king, indicating to him that he would
be safe if he (the king) would put all his hope and confidence in
God (verses 1-13). Verses 14-16 comprise the divine response, a
guarantee of protection in return for loyalty. This psalm probably comes from the court of the northern kings of Israel. Its
wording has made it a traditional night prayer of the Church.

1 Whoever dwells in the shelter of the Most High
   and passes the night in the shadow of the
            Almighty—

2 he says: "O Yahweh, my refuge, my stronghold,
   I put all my trust in you, my God."

3 He alone will set you free from the snare;
   he alone will shield you from poisoned arrows.

4 He will conceal you with his wings
   and under their shadow you will find refuge;
   his arm will be your shield and shelter.

5 You need not fear the dogs that track you by
            night,
   nor the arrow that flies by day,

6 nor the pestilence that prowls in the darkness,
   nor the plague that stalks at noon.

7 A thousand may fall to your left,
   ten thousand more go down at your right;
   but you it will never approach.

8 You have only to lift up your eyes
   to see how the wicked are repaid.

9 If you consider Yahweh as your refuge,
   if you make the Most High your support,

10 then no evil will fall upon you,
   no plague will approach your tent.

11 For he will command his angels
so they will keep you in all your ways:

12 they will bear you upon their hands
so you do not strike your foot against a stone.

13 On the lion and the viper you will tread,
and you will trample the young lion and the
serpent.

14 "If he sets his love on me,
I shall rescue him;
I shall protect him
if he professes my name.

15 When he calls, I shall answer:
'I am with you.'
I shall save him from his anguish
and give him glory.

16 He will live to be full of years
and will drink deeply of my saving power."

Psalm 92 (91)

Though there are elements of several types of psalms combined in Psalm 92 it seems in its present form to be a royal song of thanksgiving. The poem begins like a hymn (verses 2-4), then reflects on the works of Yahweh somewhat in the style of a wisdom-reflection (verses 5-10). Then the king praises God for his deliverance (verses 11-12) and concludes that the Lord will always thus favor his faithful ones (verses 13-16).

1   *A psalm; a song for the sabbath day.*

    It is good to praise you, Yahweh,
    and sing to your name, O Most High,

2   to describe your unfailing love at daybreak
    and your faithfulness through the hours of the
          night

3   to the accompaniment of zither and harp
    and the melody of a lyre.

4   Yes, Yahweh, you gladden me with what you do;
    I sing out for joy at the works of your hands.

5   How great your works are, Yahweh—
    how deep your thoughts, O Great One!

6   The brainless man does not comprehend,
    the fool does not understand

7   that, although evil men grow like weeds
    and idolaters thrive,
    he will destroy them forever and ever.

8   But you are forever exalted, O Yahweh,

9   and your enemies, Yahweh, will perish—
    they will surely perish,
    and idolaters will be scattered.

10   But you let me be like a wild ox[a] tossing its horn.
     I am anointed with fresh oil.

11   My eyes have seen the rout of those who defame
          me,
     and my ears have heard of the defeat of those evil
          assailants.

12   The just man will flourish like a palm tree
     and grow like a cedar of Lebanon.

13   Those who are transplanted to the house of
          Yahweh
     will grow vigorous in the court of our God.

14   They will still put out buds in old age;
     they will still be green and fresh,

15   so they may proclaim
     how fair Yahweh, my Mountain, is;
     there is no iniquity in him.

---

[a] A symbol of strength.

Psalm 93 (92)

A hymn celebrating the Lord's victory over the forces of chaos at the time of creation. Undoubtedly this psalm was used at the season of the fall festival when the creation was recalled and the providence of Yahweh in maintaining the order necessary for human existence was praised. Verse 1 suggests that the ceremonial of the feast renewed the kingship of the Lord; verses 2-4 recount the power of Yahweh over rebellious chaos. Verse 5 states the permanence of Yahweh's creation and that all lesser gods are (poetically pictured) forever doing Yahweh homage.

1   Yahweh is King, and appareled in majesty.
    Yahweh is clothed, and the belt he wears is
        victory.
    The world is firmly set, never again to rock,

2   Your throne was firmly set from ancient times;
    you have existed from all eternity.

3   The tides raised their roar, O Yahweh—
    they raised their roar;
    the tides raised their pounding waves.

4   Greater than the roar of the waters,
    stronger than the breakers of the sea,
    mightier than the highest heaven was Yahweh.

5   Your enthronement is all secure;
    the holy ones praise you, Yahweh,
    as long as days will last.

Psalm 94 (93)

The speaker in Psalm 94 is a public figure, a prophet or a king. The form of the psalm appears to be a composite, a lament and a thanksgiving at the same time. The psalmist describes a state of lawlessness in the realm (verses 1-15). Then he describes his own situation and how Yahweh delivered him from it (verses 16-23). Undoubtedly he was acting for the people and the Lord's rescue benefited not only the psalmist but the nation as well.

1 God of retribution, O Yahweh,
   O God of retribution, come forward now:

2 Stand up, Judge of the world,
   and award the arrogant their just deserts!

3 How much longer, Yahweh—
   how much longer will the wicked prance about?

4 How much longer will they babble
   and prattle their arrogance?
   How much longer will the idolaters jabber?

5 They crushed your people, Yahweh,
   and they afflicted your estate.

6 They killed widows and foreign minorities
   and they murdered orphans.

7 Then they declared: "Yahweh does not see
   and the God of Jacob does not watch."

8 You brainless people, learn some intelligence!
   You fools, when will you gain some wisdom?

9 Will the one who designed the ear not be listening,
   the one who fashioned the eye not be looking?

10 Will the one who disciplines nations not punish?
   Is the teacher of mankind without knowledge?

11 Yahweh knows the schemes of men,
   how they are just so much air.

12 How blest, Yahweh, is the man you teach
and instruct in your law,

13 giving him relief during the days of evil
while a pit is being dug for the wicked!

14 Yahweh will surely not forsake his people
nor will he abandon his own estate.

15 The bench of justice will surely restore fair
judgment,
and along with it every honest heart.

16 Who stood up for me against the wicked?
Who took my side against the worshippers of
idols?

17 Had Yahweh not been helping me
I would have become, in an instant,
a resident of the silence.

18 Just when I thought, "My feet are slipping,"
your unfailing love, O Yahweh, held me up.

19 Just when my worries had become too many for
me,
your consolations brought delight to my spirit.

20 Can the bench of iniquity be partners with you,
or those who incite disorder
receive your protection?

21 They assembled against the just man
and under cover of silence
condemned the innocent man.

22 But Yahweh became a fortress for me,
my God became my mountain-fastness.

23 But he made their idols turn against them,
obliterating them by their own evil.
Yahweh, our God, has obliterated them.

Psalm 95 (94)

A hymn resembling Psalms 50 and 81. Verses 1-5 invite the congregation to worship Yahweh, the Creator. Elements that other peoples thought of as gods (the sea, mountain heights, etc.) are called creatures of the Lord here. Verses 6-7 recall that Yahweh is likewise God of the covenant, and verses 8-11 remind the people that the first beneficiaries of the covenant were faithless and stubborn even during the wandering in the desert and at the oases of Meribah ("the place of discord") and Massah ("day of testing"). A like fate could overtake contemporary members of God's people unless their response to the divine goodness is better than the conduct of their fathers. The psalm was undoubtedly used during the fall festival when creation was recalled and the covenant was renewed.

1 Come, let us sing our joy to Yahweh.
  Let us acclaim the Rock who saves us!

2 Let us come into his presence giving thanks
  and acclaim him with songs of praise!

3 Yahweh is a mighty God,
  he is the Great King over all the gods.

4 The deep places of the world below he holds in his
      hand
  and his are the heights of the mountains.

5 The sea is his, for he made it,
  and the dry land fashioned by his hands.

6 Come, bow before him in worship,
  kneel before Yahweh who created us,

7 for he is our God;
  we are the people he shepherds
  and the flock of his pasture.

  If only you would hear his voice today:
8 "Do not be obstinate
  as you were in that place of discord,
  on that day of testing in the desert,

9   when your fathers challenged me,
     when they tried me
     even after they had seen the wonders I could do.

10   "For forty years I loathed that generation;
     I said: 'They are a people with hearts gone astray;
     these are not the people who acknowledge my
          dominion.'

11   So, in anger I swore an oath:
     they will never reach my place of rest."

Psalm 96 (95)

A hymn for the festival celebrating the enthronement of Yahweh as king. The song recalls Yahweh's creation victory (verses 1-5). Verses 6-10 picture a theophany, a manifestation of the divine presence in the temple, some of which was probably acted out in the course of the liturgical worship. Verses 11-13 take up again a renewed creation motif, which probably is meant to look forward to the time when Yahweh would make his reign over all the earth manifest.

1 Sing a new song to Yahweh!
All people on earth, sing to Yahweh!

2 Sing to Yahweh and praise his name!
Day after day proclaim his victory.

3 Among the nations tell of his glory.
To all the nations recount his marvelous deeds.

4 Great is Yahweh, worthy of all praise is the
Mighty One.
More than all gods is he to be feared.

5 For the gods of the peoples are only idols.
But Yahweh made the heavens.

6 Majesty and splendor attend him;
in his sanctuary are power and beauty.

7 Families of nations, give glory and praise to
Yahweh!
Give Yahweh glory and praise!

8 Give glory to the name of Yahweh!
Bring an offering and enter his court;

9 in holy vestments bow down before Yahweh;
tremble before him, all the earth.

10 Proclaim among the nations: "Yahweh is king."
He has made the world firm in its place,
it will never totter.
He will judge the peoples with equity.

11   Let the heavens rejoice and earth be glad!
      Let the sea thunder,
      and all the creatures that live in it!

12   Let the fields be overjoyed,
      and all that grows in them!

      Let all the trees of the forest
      sing for joy (13) before Yahweh;
      he is coming to rule the earth!

      He will rule all the world with justice
      and the peoples with his faithfulness.

Psalm 97 (96)

A hymn for the enthronement feast of Yahweh. The song begins with the announcement of Yahweh's kingship, followed by a description of the theophany (verses 1-6). Yahweh's superiority to the idols worshipped by nations more powerful than Israel is described, along with the coming rewards reserved for the faithful people of the Lord (verses 7-11). Verse 12 concludes the poem with a call to praise frequently used at the autumnal festival.

1 Yahweh is king!
Let the land rejoice, and all the islands[a] be glad!

2 Clouds and thunderheads surround him;
justice and equity are the platform of his throne.

3 Fire marches before his face;
it blazes behind his back.

4 His lightning illumines the world.
Earth sees it and starts to shake:

5 The mountains melt like wax at the sight of
Yahweh,
the Sovereign of the whole earth.

6 The skies announce the justice of his claim;
all the peoples see his glory.

7 Let all who are the slaves of carved images be
ashamed:
all those who boast of their powerless idols.
Bow down before him, all you gods!

8 Let Zion hear and be glad;
let the daughters of Judah rejoice
because of those acts of yours, Yahweh, which
establish justice.

---

a These "islands" included, in Israelite geography, Europe and Africa, known to Phoenician sailors.

9 You, Yahweh, are surely the Most High over all
    the earth,
  higher by far than all the gods.

10 Yahweh loves those who hate evil:
  he guards the lives of those who are devoted to
    him;
  he will rescue them from the grasp of evil men.

11 A garden of delights is reserved for the just
  and happiness for the upright of heart.

12 Be glad in Yahweh, you just people,
  and give praise to his holy name!

Psalm 98 (97)

A hymn of Yahweh's kingship. This song is another of those hymns for the new year festival which celebrate the renewal of the Lord's victory over chaos (verses 1-2) and his covenant mercy to Israel (verse 3). Verses 4-9 bring all creation into the liturgical celebration, looking forward to the final establishment of Yahweh's reign over the whole earth.

1   *A psalm.*

    Sing a new song to Yahweh
    for he has done marvelous deeds;
    his right hand and his holy arm have won him
        victory.

2   Yahweh has made his victory known;
    he has displayed his justice while the nations
        looked on.

3   Remember, house of Israel,
    his love and faithfulness.
    All the ends of the earth
    see the victory of our God.

4   Acclaim Yahweh, all the earth;
    break into joyful songs of praise!

5   Play the harp in honor of Yahweh;
    play the harp and the strings.

6   With trumpets and sound of the horn
    acclaim Yahweh, the King!

7   Let the sea thunder and all that live in it;
    the world and all who dwell in it.

8   Let the rivers clap their hands;
    let the hills all sing for joy

9   at the presence of Yahweh,
    for he comes to establish his will on the earth.

    He establishes his will in the world with justice
    and among the peoples with fairness.

Psalm 99 (98)

Another psalm of the enthronement of Yahweh. The chief characteristics of this psalm are its emphasis on the holiness of the Lord and the necessity of the priestly intercessors in Israel's religious life. After proclaiming the kingship and power of the Lord (verses 1-2) the poet calls on all to recognize the sovereignty of Yahweh (verses 3-5). Then he connects the contemporary priesthood with the great priests of Israel's earlier dealings with the Lord (verses 6-8) and concludes with a final call to praise (verse 9).

1   Yahweh is King!
    Let the people tremble!

    He is enthroned on the Cherubim!
    Let spasms of fear rock the earth!

2   Yahweh is too great for Zion,
    exalted far beyond all the peoples.

3   Let them praise your Name
    for you are great and awesome!
    "He is holy!"

4   You are the mightiest of kings and you love
            justice.
    You it was—you established equity;
    you it was—you brought judgment and justice to
            Jacob.

5   Praise Yahweh, our God, to high heaven
    and bow down before the cushion of his feet!
    "He is holy!"

6   There is still a Moses, still an Aaron among his
            priests.
    There is still a Samuel
    among those who call upon his Name.
    They call upon Yahweh and he still answers them.

7 From the pillar of cloud God still speaks.
   They keep his commandments
   and the law he gives them.

8 Yahweh, our God, you still answer them,
   and to them you are a forgiving God;
   but you still deal sternly with them
   as the Vindicator Most High.

9 Praise Yahweh, our God, to high heaven
   and bow down before his holy mountain!
   "Yes, Yahweh, our God, is holy!"

Psalm 100 (99)

A hymn of thanksgiving and praise. Though this poem does not mention the kingship of Yahweh in so many words, its position here at the end of a series of enthronement psalms suggests that Psalm 100 too is a hymn for the festival of Yahweh's kingship. Verse 3 speaks of the creation-covenant theme and verse 4 of a solemn procession. The psalm was probably used at the new year festival in the autumn.

1   *A psalm for giving thanks.*

    Shout for joy to Yahweh, all the earth!

2   Serve[a] Yahweh with happiness.
    Come into his presence with a joyful song!

3   Acknowledge that Yahweh is God!
    He made us when we were nothing.
    We are his people and the flock he shepherds.

4   Enter his gates giving thanks;
    praise him as you come into his court!
    Give thanks to him and bless his name!

5   How good Yahweh is!
    His unfailing love will last forever;
    his faithfulness, age after age.

---

a   "Serve": the word here means specifically "worship", "celebrate the liturgy for . . ."

Psalm 101 (100)

A royal psalm. What seems unique about this psalm is that in it
and by means of it a king is examining his conscience in public.
The speaker who is doubtless a king apparently used such a
ritual as this psalm is to publicly proclaim his religious intentions toward his subjects. Beginning with a declaration of
praises to God (verses 1 and 2) the psalmist pronounces his own
innocence of idolatry (verses 2b-3) and then promises to rid his
domains of idolators and those unfaithful to the covenant
(verses 4-8).

1   *A psalm of David.*

    Your unfailing love and fair judgment I sing.
    I play music for you, Yahweh,

2   and I sing of your complete dominion.
    When will you come to me?

    I walk in my palace with undivided heart.

3   I do not set the oracles of worthless idols
        before my eyes.
    I loathe image-making so that it has no hold on
        me.

4   The unruly heart turns away from me.
    I am not the friend of evil men.

5   I shut those out who slander their neighbors in
        secret.
    I cannot stand the man with arrogant eyes
        and proud heart.[a]

6   My eyes favor the faithful in the land.
    The one who may minister to me
    is the man who walks the way of honesty.

---

[a] Though the connection is not entirely clear, the terms used in this verse
(such as "slander", "man with arrogant eyes" and "proud heart") seem to
refer to idolaters.

7 The maker of deceitful idols
   does not live in my house;
   the man who speaks falsehood
   does not remain in my sight.

8 Day after day I will expel all the wicked men of
        the land;
   I will excommunicate every worshipper of idols
   from the city of Yahweh.

Psalm 102 (101)

Though the nature of this psalm has been much disputed, it seems best to regard it as the prayer of a Jerusalem king made under great distress. The historical circumstances which prompted the composition of such a poem as this cannot be determined. Probably the psalm was once part of the cult: the king prayed for the prosperity both of himself and his kingdom before his annual enthronement celebration. He describes his situation as besieged by drought (verses 2-12). He utters his confidence in the deliverance of Yahweh (verses 13-23). In verses 24-29 he reviews the situation again and once again repeats his faith in the ultimate victory of the Lord.

1   *Prayer of a poor person when he is worn out and is pouring out his complaint before Yahweh.*

2   Yahweh, listen to my prayer
    and let my plea come before you.

3   Do not hide your face from me on the day of my
        anguish.
    Turn your ear toward me;
    on the day I call, answer me quickly.

4   My days are disappearing faster than smoke
    and my bones are burning up as if in an oven.

5   Scorched like stubble, my heart has completely
        dried up:
    I am dried up by Death, who devours all.

6   My jaws ache with my groaning;
    my bones are visible right through my wasted
        flesh.

7   I am like a vulture out in the desert,
    like an owl in the wilds.

8   I am restless and like a sparrow,
    like a bird that twitters on the roof all day long.

9   My enemy taunts me:
    Death mocks me as he feasts on me.

10   Ashes are my food
     and from my tears I draw my drink.

11   In your anger and wrath
     you picked me up to hurl me down.

12   My days are like lengthening shadows
     and I am withering away like the stubble.

13   But you, O Yahweh, are enthroned from eternity
     and your glory endures through all the ages.

14   You will rise up and show compassion to Zion
     because it is time to pity her.
     Yes, the time appointed is here.

15   How fond your servants are of her stones!
     How her dust moves them to pity!

16   The nations will acknowledge your name, Yahweh,
     and all the kingdoms of earth will reverence your
       glory

17   when Yahweh builds up Zion again,
     when he appears to her in his glory,

18   when he attends to the prayer of the destitute
     and no longer ignores their plea.

19   Let this be written for the generation that is to
       come,
     so that a people still to be created
     may praise Yahweh.

20   "He looked down from his sacred heights;
     from heaven Yahweh surveyed the earth

21   to hear the sighing of prisoners
     and unchain those under sentence of death.

22   Then might the name 'Yahweh' be proclaimed in
       Zion
     and his praise in Jerusalem,

23   when peoples and kingdoms
       gather together to serve him."

24   Yahweh diminished my strength by his own
            decision
       and shortened my days.

25   I say: "Do not take me away before half my days
            are over,
       while your own years go on age after age."

26   Long ago you laid the foundations of the earth
       and the heavens are the work of your hands.

27   They will perish but you will remain.
       All of them will wear out like clothing.
       You change them like clothes and they fade away.

28   But you remain the same
       and your years will never come to an end.

29   The children of your servants will dwell in safety
       and the place of their descendants
       will be secure in your presence.

Psalm 103 (102)

A triumphant hymn of praise to Yahweh, Lord of the covenant and Creator and Ruler of all creatures. The psalmist, speaking undoubtedly for the whole congregation, begins with praises from himself for the Lord, his Benefactor (verses 1-5). Then he praises Yahweh as Israel's covenant-partner (verses 6-14). All people are recalled in verses 15-18. Finally (verses 19-22) all the beings of creation are included in an invitation to join the poet in praising the Lord.

1   *Of David.*

   Bless Yahweh, my soul!
   Bless his holy name, all my being!

2   Bless Yahweh, my soul,
   and do not forget all the favors he has done:

3   he forgives all your guilt
   and heals all your diseases;

4   he redeems your life from the Pit
   and crowns you with unfailing love and mercy;

5   he fills your eternity with goodness
   when your youth will be renewed
   like that of a phoenix.

6   Yahweh executes justice and fair judgment
   for all the oppressed.

7   He made his ways known to Moses
   and showed the sons of Israel what he could do.

8   Tender and gracious is Yahweh,
   slow to anger but rich in unfailing love.

9   He is not constantly finding fault
   nor forever nursing a grudge.

10   He does not deal with us as our sins deserve
   nor does he repay us in accordance with our guilt.

11 Indeed as high as heaven is above the nether-
world,
   so is his unfailing love for those who reverence
him.

12 As far as the east is from the west,
   he has put our rebellious actions away from us.

13 As a father is tender toward his children
Yahweh is tender toward those who reverence
him.

14 He knows very well what form we have
and remembers we are but clay.

15 Man—what are his days but hay?
A wild flower—that is all his blossoming.

16 If a wind blows over him, he is no more
and the place where he was knows him no longer.

17 But Yahweh's unfailing love is from eternity
and it will last into eternity
for those who reverence him.
His generosity too will last
for their children's children

18 who keep the covenant with him,
remembering to observe its terms.

19 Yahweh set his throne in the heavens
but his royal dominion extends over all things.

20 Bless Yahweh, you angels of his,
mighty warriors who heed his commands,
who listen for the sound of his orders!

21 Bless Yahweh, you armies of his,
the attendants who carry out his wishes!

22 Bless Yahweh, you works of his,
all subjects of his everywhere!
Bless Yahweh, my soul!

Psalm 104 (103)

A royal hymn to the Creator of all things. Many scholars have noted the resemblance of Psalm 104 to an Egyptian hymn to the sun god attributed to Pharaoh Amen-hotep IV (ca. 1375-1357 B.C.) also known as Ikhnaton. Probably this hymn or poems based upon it were known to Canaanite poets and through them came also to the attention of Israelite psalmists. However that may be, Psalm 104 has a theology that is distinctly Israelite. It attributes all creation to Yahweh, even the sun and moon which were worshipped by pagans as gods. It states that all life depends on the Lord (verses 29-30) and concludes with the king's wish that all sinners may be removed from his realm.

1 Praise Yahweh, O my soul!
   Yahweh, my God,
      you are great and of surpassing greatness!
   You are arrayed in splendor and majesty!

2 He is clothed with the sun for raiment
   and he spread the heavens out like a tent.

3 He stored the waters in his upper chambers
   and placed his chariot on the dark clouds.
   He walks upon the outspread wings of Cherubim.

4 He makes the winds his messengers
   and fire and flames his attendants.

5 He set the earth firmly on its pilings,
   so that it could never totter again.

6 You covered it with the ocean as with a garment;
   the water stood higher than the mountains.

7 When you roared at them they fled;
   they ran away from the crash of your thunder.

8 They went up into the mountains,
   down into the canyons—
      the places you had appointed for them.

9   You determined the boundaries they were not to
        cross,
    to keep them from coming back again to cover
        the earth.

10   You commissioned springs and torrents
    to run between the mountains.

11   They supply water for all wild animals
    and wild asses can satisfy their thirst.

12   On their banks dwell the birds of the sky;
    from the dense foliage they sing their songs.

13   He waters the mountains from his upper
        chambers:
    the earth is replete
    with the supplies from his storehouses.

14   He makes grass grow for the cattle,
    for the animals which plow the soil.

    He also brings bread from the earth
15   and wine to warm the heart of man.
    With oil he gives him a healthy look
    and with bread he sustains his heart.

16   He drenches the trees of Yahweh,
    the cedars of Lebanon, which he planted.

17   There the sparrow builds its nest.
    In the junipers the stork has its home.

18   The high mountains are for wild goats
    and the crags form dens for badgers.

19   The moon changes according to phases:
    the sun knows its times for setting.

20   It gets dark and night comes on
    and all the animals of the forest go on the prowl.

21   The lion cubs growl for prey,
    begging their food from God.

22 The sun comes up and they slink away
   to stretch out once again in their dens.

23 Man goes out to his labor
   to farm until evening comes.

24 How diverse are the things you have made, O
      Yahweh!
   You made all of them with wisdom;
   the earth is filled with your creatures!

25 He is God of the sea,
   towering and broad of reach;
   he made countless things that swim—
   living things large and small.

26 He made ships for voyaging;
   he molded Leviathan just to amuse himself.

27 All of them look expectantly to you,
   to give them their food at the right time.

28 When you give it to them, they gather it up;
   when you open your hand, O Kindly One,
   they are satisfied with good things.

29 If you turn your face away, they begin to expire;
   if you withdraw your spirit, they gasp their last
   and back they go to their clay.

30 Send out your spirit, and they will be created
      again
   and you will renew the face of the earth.

31 Forever may the glory of Yahweh endure!
   May Yahweh be glad for what he has made.

32 Under his gaze the earth trembles;
   at his touch the mountains give off smoke.

33 I would sing to Yahweh as long as I live;
   I would sing praise to my God while I have being.

34 When my plea is admitted to his presence,
I will have joy in Yahweh.

35 Let sinners disappear from the land.
Let the wicked live no longer!
Praise Yahweh, O my soul!

Halleluia.

Psalm 105 (104)

An historical psalm composed for a festival of the renewal of the covenant. This poem reviews the dealings of God with Abraham and his tribe, with the Joseph tradition of Israel's entrance into Egypt, and with the events surrounding the exodus from the "land of Ham" under Moses. It concludes with only passing references to the desert sojourn and the entrance into the promised land. There is no mention of the bitter times of trial in the wilderness nor of the giving of the law at Mount Sinai. Probably this poem was composed under the influence of the Elohist theology, the spirituality of the northern kingdom of Israel in its earlier period.

1 Thank Yahweh and call upon his name!
   Make his actions known among the peoples.

2 Sing to him and play music to him;
   write songs about all his wonders.

3 Glory in his holy name, and let your hearts be
      glad,
   all of you that seek Yahweh.

4 Look for Yahweh and his strength
   and seek his presence always.

5 Call to mind the miracles he has done
   and his wonders and the judgments he has spoken.

6 Listen, descendants of his servant Abraham,
   children of Jacob, his chosen one.

7 He is Yahweh, our God,
   whose rule extends over all the earth.

8 Forever he remembers the covenant he made,
   the agreement he ordered for a thousand
      generations:

9 that covenant he concluded with Abraham,
   the oath he swore to Isaac,

10 the decree he confirmed for Jacob,
his everlasting covenant with Israel,

11 when he said: "To you I shall give the land;
Canaan will be your estate in the hills."

12 They were a small population,
a mere handful, a nomadic minority in the land.

13 While they wandered from nation to nation
and to one kingdom after another,

14 he allowed no man to oppress them.
He rebuked kings because of them:

15 "Do not touch my anointed ones—
do no harm to my prophets!"

16 Then he invoked a famine on the land,
breaking every stalk of grain.

17 He sent a man ahead of them,
Joseph sold as a slave.

18 They forced his feet into irons,
and his neck was put into an iron collar,

19 until the word of Yahweh came to him
and Yahweh's promise came true.

20 He sent the king to release him,
commanded the ruler of peoples to set him free.

21 He made him the master of his house
and ruler of all his possessions.

22 He instructed his officials himself
and taught his elders wisdom.

23 So Israel entered Egypt,
and Jacob became a foreign minority in the land
of Ham.

24   The Great One made his people abound,
and they became too numerous for their
adversaries.

25   He turned their hearts to hate his people
and to begin double-dealing with his servants.

26   He sent Moses, his servant,
and Aaron, whom he had chosen.

27   They performed his miracles in that wilderness;
they worked his wonders in the land of Ham.[a]

28   He sent darkness and it grew so dark
that they could not see his deeds.

29   He changed their waters into blood
and caused their fish to die.

30   He commanded frogs to swarm over their land,
right into the apartment of their king.

31   At his word came flies
and there were gnats everywhere within their
borders.

32   He gave them hail instead of showers
and he made lightning flash over their land.

33   He put a blight on their grapes and figs
and splintered the trees on their hillsides.

34   At his word came the locusts,
grasshoppers beyond all counting,

35   and they devoured every blade of grass
throughout the land,
and consumed all the produce of the soil.

36   He struck down every firstborn in Egypt
and the first fruits of all their vigor.

---

a "Ham": an alternative name for Egypt.

37 Then he led them out with silver and gold,
and among his tribes
there was no one who stumbled.

38 Egypt was glad at their exodus
because dread of Israel had fallen on them.

39 He spread out a cloud to screen them
and a fire to illumine the night.

40 They begged and he had the quails come
and he satisfied them with the bread of heaven.

41 He opened a rock and water gushed out
and flowed like a river in the desert,

42 because he had recalled the sacred pledge
which he had made to Abraham, his servant.

43 And he led his people out amid rejoicing;
he led his chosen ones out amid shouts of joy.

44 And he gave them the lands of the nations
and they impounded the wealth of the peoples,

45 for as long as they would keep his commandments
and observe his laws.

Psalm 106 (105)

Psalm 106 is composed with the theology of the Book of Deuteronomy in mind. It is a national confession of sinfulness, recalling the rebelliousness of Israel especially during the exodus and at the time of the conquest of the land. The psalm admits that Israel is as guilty now as she was then (verse 6) and prays for a return from exile (verse 47). From these verses scholars infer that Psalm 106 dates in its present form at least from the period after the exile. Verses 1-5 form an introduction, verse 6 sets the tone, verses 7-46 review the story of Israel's ingratitude after Yahweh had rescued them from Egypt, and verse 47 is a final prayer. Verse 48 does not belong to the psalm proper but is merely a doxology indicating that the fourth book of the psalter is at an end.

1   Halleluia.

   Thank Yahweh because he is good
   and because his unfailing love will last forever.

2   Who could express the power of Yahweh?
   Who could sound all his praises?

3   How blest is the man who cherishes what is right:
   the man who acts justly at all times!

4   Remember me, Yahweh, in your mighty love.
   Visit me with your saving power.

5   Then I too can experience the kindness
   you show toward your chosen ones,
   I too can be glad with the gladness of your nation
   and glory in your inheritance.

6   We have sinned as much as our fathers;
   we too have made ourselves guilty,
   we too have committed crimes.

7 After Egypt our fathers did not comprehend
  your wonderful acts;
  they did not keep in mind
  the richness of your unfailing love.

  After the Sea of Reeds
  they rebelled against the Most High,
8 though he had saved them because of his Name
  so that he could manifest his power.

9 He rebuked the Sea, and he dried up the reeds,
  and he let them walk through the deep
  as through the desert.

10 He saved them from the hand of the enemy
  and redeemed them from the hand of the foe.

11 The waters covered their adversaries
  and there was not a single survivor.

12 Then they put faith in his promises
  and they sang his praises.

13 They were quick to forget his works;
  they would not wait for his advice.

14 They grumbled bitterly in the desert
  and they tested God, out in the barren waste.

15 But he granted them their request
  and removed the empty feeling inside them.

16 Then they grew envious of Moses in the camp,
  jealous of Aaron, who was sacred to Yahweh.

17 The earth opened and swallowed up Dathan
  and closed over the clique of Abiram.

18 Fire blazed up against their faction,
  enkindling the wicked in the flames.

19 They fashioned a calf at Horeb
  and bowed low before an image of cast metal.

20 They bartered their God of glory
   for the statue of a grass-eating ox!

21 They forgot God, their Savior,
   who had done great marvels in Egypt,

22 wonders in the land of Ham,
   and frightening feats at the Sea of Reeds.

23 Then he decided to devastate them—
   except that Moses, his chosen one,
   took his stand between him and his people
   to restrain his rage from destroying them.

24 Then they spurned the Land that was desirable
   and refused to believe in his promises.

25 They grew recalcitrant in their tents,
   not listening to the voice of Yahweh.

26 So he raised his hand against them
   to strike them down there in the wilderness,

27 to disperse their descendants among the peoples
   and scatter them among the countries.

28 But they yoked themselves to Baal of Peor
   and ate the banquets of the dead.

29 They irritated him so with their doings
   that a plague finally broke out among them.

30 Then Phinehas intervened
   and the plague was brought under control,

31 and this has been written down in his favor
   and regarded as virtue forever, throughout the
       ages.

32 They provoked him to anger at the waters of
       Meribah,
   and it went badly with Moses because of them,

33 because they resisted his spirit
so that he spoke impetuously.

34 They did not exterminate the peoples
as Yahweh had ordered them,

35 but they intermarried with the Gentiles
and acquired their habits.

36 They served their idols
and these became an enticement for them.

37 They sacrificed their sons and their daughters
to demons.

38 They poured out innocent blood,
the blood of their own sons and daughters
whom they had sacrificed to the idols of
Canaan—
in that way they desecrated the land
with rivers of blood!

39 They defiled themselves with their actions
and committed adultery by their deeds.

40 Then the anger of Yahweh blazed up against his
people,
and he grew disgusted with his inheritance.

41 He handed them over to the nations
and those who hated them became their rulers.

42 Their foes repressed them
and they were debased under their hands.

43 Time after time he would rescue them,
but they became more firm in their intentions,
and so they pined away in their guilt.

44 Still, he would see them in their anguish,
whenever he heard their cry.

45 He would recall his covenant with them
and lead them in the richness of his unfailing love.

46 He showed them great tenderness,
   right there in the sight of their captors.

47 Save us, Yahweh, our God,
   and gather us in from among the nations,
   so we can give thanks to your holy name,
   which is to be glorified wherever you are praised.

48 Praise Yahweh, the God of Israel,
   from eternity to eternity,
   and let all the people say: "Amen!"

   Halleluia.

Psalm 107 (106)

A public song of thanksgiving. This psalm, after a brief introduction (verses 1-3) clearly falls into five parts. There are four invitations to render praise to the Lord, (verses 4-7, 10-14, 17-20, and 23-30), made to groups who owed special gratitude to Yahweh: people saved from the wilderness, from imprisonment, from sickness, and from the sea. The fifth and final part of the psalm (verses 33-43) reminds Israel of how prosperity follows the nation which humbly follows the will of the Lord while the proud are afflicted by drought and want. This last section of the psalm closes (verse 43) with an admonition delivered in the style of the wisdom teachers. The various sections of the psalm are separated from one another by a recurring refrain.

1 Thank Yahweh because he is good
  and because his unfailing love will last forever.

2 Let those redeemed by Yahweh
  tell how he redeemed them
  from the hands of the oppressor,

3 how he gathered them in from the countries,
  from the east and from the west,
  from the north and from the southern sea.

4 They wandered in the wilderness,
  tramping through the barren wastelands
  without finding a city to dwell in.

5 They were hungry, they were thirsty,
  their vitality grew less and less.

6 But in their anguish
  they called out to Yahweh for help
  and he rescued them from their hardships.

7 Then he guided them by the shortest way
  until they came to a city to dwell in.

8   Let them acknowledge to Yahweh
     the unfailing love he has shown them
     and the wonders he has done
     for the children of men.

9   He satisfied their gnawing hunger
     and filled their hungry throats
     with good things to eat.

10   There were those who dwelt in darkness and
        shadow,
     bound by torture and chains,

11   because they had defied the commands of God
     and flouted the counsel of the Most High.

12   He subdued their spirit through troubles:
     they stumbled because there was no one to help
        them.

13   But in their anguish
     they called out to Yahweh for help
     and he rescued them from their hardships.

14   He brought them out of darkness and shadow
     and he snapped open their bonds.

15   Let them acknowledge to Yahweh
     the unfailing love he has shown them
     and the wonders he has done
     for the children of men.

16   He smashed in bronze doors
     and shattered iron locks.

17   There were those
     who were enervated by their rebellious ways
     and tortured because of their guilty deeds.

18   They were so nauseated by any kind of food
     that they had reached the Gates of Death.

19 But in their anguish
they called out to Yahweh for help
and he rescued them from their hardships.

20 He sent his word and it healed them
and he brought them relief from their sickness.

21 Let them acknowledge to Yahweh
the unfailing love he has shown them
and the wonders he has done
for the children of men.

22 Let them offer sacrifices of thanksgiving
and recount his deeds with cries of joy.

23 There are those who cross the sea in ships,
engaging in trade across the mighty waters.

24 They have seen the deeds
and wonders of Yahweh in the deeps.

25 He has merely to speak and the wind begins to
rise—
a storm, that lifts the waves high.

26 They rise to the heavens, they go down to the
depths,
their throats run dry at the danger.

27 They pitch and toss like drunken men
and all their skill is exhausted.

28 But in their anguish they call out to Yahweh for
help
and he guides them out of their hardships.

29 He stills the storm to a mere whisper
and the violent waves are brought to stillness.

30 They are glad because of the calm
when he pilots them to their port of commerce.

31 Let them acknowledge to Yahweh
the unfailing love he has shown them
and the wonders he has done for the children of
men.

32 Let them extol him in the assembly of the people
and praise him in the session of the elders.

33 He changed rivers back into desert
and springs into parched soil.

34 He turned fruitful land into salt flats
because of the wickedness of its population.

35 He changed the desert into ponds of water
and parched soil into springs;

36 he settled a starving people there
and they founded a city to dwell in.

37 They sowed fields and planted vineyards,
and they harvested a plentiful crop.

38 He blessed them
and their population greatly increased
and he did not allow their cattle to decrease.

39 But oppression and tragedy and mourning
did decrease
and even depart from them.

40 The one who showed his contempt for nobles
and made them wander in a trackless waste—

41 he is the same one
who lifted the poor up to a safe dwelling
and treated their clans like a flock.

42 Let upright men see this and be glad,
but let evil men close their mouths.

43 Whoever is wise will ponder all this
and he will discern the unfailing love of Yahweh.

Psalm 108 (107)

Psalm 108 is either a compilation (with only slight variations) of Psalm 57:8-11 and Psalm 60:7-14, or it is dependent on the same sources which were used in composing those psalms. The reasons behind this apparent doublet in the psalter have not yielded themselves to research. The notes on Psalms 57 and 60 will give the background behind Psalm 108.

1   *A song; a psalm of David.*

2   This I have determined, O God:
    to sing and play music with all my being:

3   Awake, harp and lyre!
    I would awaken the dawn!

4   I would thank you, Yahweh, among the peoples;
    I would play music to you among the nations!

5   High as the heavens is your unfailing love,
    high as the clouds, your faithfulness.

6   You tower above the heavens, O God,
    high above all the earth is your glory.

7   Let your right hand bring us victory
    so that your beloved people may be rescued.

8   God made a pronouncement from his sanctuary:
    "Gladly I take Shechem for my portion
    and measure off the Valley of Succoth.

9   To me falls Gilead, Manasseh falls to me;
    Ephraim is my helmet, Judah my mace.

10 Moab is my washbowl,
    Edom the property I claim when I plant my boot.
    Over Philistia I shout in victory."

11 Who will bring me to Petra?
    Who will set me on Edom's throne?

12 Will you, O God, stay angry at us
and never again march out with our armies?

13 Bring us aid against those who assail us,
because there is no hope for deliverance by man.

14 With God we will do mighty deeds;
he himself will trample our adversaries.

Psalm 109 (108)

The genre of this psalm is the subject of much disagreement. It appears to be the prayer of a king, assailed by bitter opponents. But some hold that it is the lament of a private individual who has been falsely accused. In verses 1-5 the poet describes his situation, but unfortunately in terms that leave us far from certain as to what it is. Verses 6-20 are a series of imprecations and curses unparalleled in the Old Testament. Scholars are divided over whether these verses are the poet's original sentiments or whether he is quoting the adversaries who have attacked him. In either case they are problematical for the Christian because verse 20 declares that the psalmist would see his adversary punished in the manner described by the foregoing lines. Verses 21-31 turn to Yahweh with pleading for the psalmist in his desperation.

1 *For the director: a psalm of David.*

   My God, do not be deaf to my hymn of praise.

2 How wide the mouths of evil and deceit are
           opened against me;
   they pursue me with lying tongues;

3 with whispers of hatred they surround me.
   They attack me for no reason:

4 in return for my love they are hostile even to me.
   They use my own prayers against me.

5 They repay my kindness with evil, my love with
           hatred.

6 Let a wicked man be his advocate,
   a prosecutor stand at his side.

7 When he is judged, let him be condemned
   and even his appeal be considered a crime.

8 May his days be few
   and his position go to another.

9   Let his children become orphans
    and his wife a widow.

10 Let his children be vagrants and beggars forever,
    their homes hounded by appraisers.

11 Let the creditor repossess everything he owns;
    let strangers loot all his earnings.

12 Let there be no one who shows him loyalty,
    none who takes pity on his orphans.

13 Let his future be cut short,
    his name disappearing in the next generation.

14 May the guilt of his father be recorded before
        Yahweh,
    and the sin of his mother not be erased.

15 May they be constantly in Yahweh's presence
    so that he wipes their memory from the earth.

16 He did not remember to show loyalty:
    he hounds the one who is poor and needy
    and tries to kill the broken-hearted man.

17 He loved cursing, and now it has come to him!
    He took no delight in blessing,
    and now it has left him far behind!

18 Cursing was as close to him as his clothing;
    it seeped into his heart like water,
    into his bones like oil.

19 So let it envelop him like a cape,
    like a sash that he ties on every day.

20 In the same way, Yahweh,
    punish those a hundred times who slander me,
    those who accuse me of evil.

21 Work a wonder in my behalf, O Yahweh, my
         Soverign Lord.
   For the sake of your Name,
   for the sake of your good Name,
   rescue me by your unfailing love.

22 How needy and poor am I,
   and my heart is broken.

23 Like a shadow I am fading and passing away:
   I have aged—my youth is gone.

24 My knees are shaky from fasting—
   my body has grown gaunt with loss of weight.

   To those who meet me,
25 I am an object of abuse;
   they shake their heads when they see me.

26 Help me, Yahweh, my God;
   save me because of your unfailing love.

27 Let them know that it is by your hand—
   that you yourself, Yahweh, have taken action.

28 Let them curse, but you bless!
   Let them rise up, but then be humiliated,
   and let your servant be glad!

29 May my adversaries put on disgrace.
   May they wear shame as if it were clothing!

30 I will voice my profound thanks to Yahweh,
   and even among the elders I will praise him,

31 because he stands at the side of the poor man
   to save his life from his judges.

Psalm 110 (109)

Of this psalm Saint Augustine wrote that it is "short in the number of its words, but a heavyweight in what it has to say" (*Enar. in Psal. 109*). Modern commentators would undoubtedly agree with the great Doctor of the Church, and would certainly add that it contains more mysteries than its length would indicate. This poem is a royal psalm, probably used in a court ritual. Generally scholars would agree on this hypothesis, but there concord ends and controversy begins. The present translation (which owes much to the notes of Fr. Mitchell Dahood on this psalm in the Anchor Bible, vol. 3, pp. 112-120) assumes that the poem was used to celebrate a victory of both Yahweh and the king. Whether this victory was a military one or whether it was a ritual one, a celebration of the cosmic victory of Yahweh, is hard to say. The court poet or priest or prophet recited the psalm to the king in the form of an oracle, assuring the king that it was Yahweh who gave him victory (verses 1-3), and that Yahweh has made a priest in the established order of Melchizedek, the former king of Jerusalem who was according to Genesis 14:18-19 also a priest of the Most High God (verse 4). Verses 5 and 6 speak of Yahweh's victory, very possibly over the forces of chaos, while the final verse speaks of the legitimacy of the king in his position as stemming from God himself. It must be admitted that all translations of this psalm are uncertain and subject to revision as new facts from the ancient Near East become known.

1   *A psalm of David.*

> This is Yahweh's oracle to my Sovereign Lord:
> "Ascend your throne at my right hand!
> I am making your foes into a chair for you,
> a cushion under your feet."

2   He has forged the scepter of your victorious
>   power;
> Yahweh of Zion has hammered it out.
>
> In battle with your foes

3   he has been your Mighty One,
     your Valiant One on the day of your conquest.

     When the Holy One appeared,
     he comforted you;
     he was the dawn of life for you,
     the dew of your youth.

4   Yahweh has sworn and will not change his mind:
     you are a priest forever according to the order of
       Melchizedek.

5   The Sovereign Lord is at your right hand;
     he struck kings on the day of his anger.

6   He put nations to flight;
     he piled up corpses
     and heads he struck far and wide.

7   He who gives inheritance
     has given him his throne;
     the God of Truth causes him to hold his head
       high.

Psalm 111 (110)

A hymn of praise in the form of an alphabetical acrostic. Each verse of the poem begins with a new letter of the Hebrew alphabet in its proper order. Since the poem seems to refer to various events of the exodus, perhaps the song was to inculcate praise for God's deliverance of his people in the mind of the singer. There is an overtone of wisdom in the psalm, evident in verses 2 and 10. On just which occasions this hymn was meant to be used is not clear from the text.

1   Halleluia.

   I will thank Yahweh with all my heart
   in the council of upright men and in the assembly.

2   Great are the works of Yahweh!
   They should be studied by all who delight in
         them.

3   All he does is splendid and glorious;
   his generosity stands firm forever.

4   He has made a memorial with his wonders.
   Yahweh is merciful and kind:

5   he provided food for those who worshipped him.
   His covenant from of old he remembered.

6   With his deeds he showed his power to his people,
   giving the Gentiles' inheritance to them.

7   The works he does are just and faithful,
   and all his commands can be trusted;

8   founded for eternity and beyond,
   they are made of fairness and truth.

9   To his people he sent redemption;
   he decreed a covenant that is forever.
   His Name is awesome and holy!

10 Reverence for Yahweh is the beginning of wisdom.
God who is good
will give understanding to all
who strive for it.
May his praise endure through eternity.

Psalm 112 (111)

Another acrostic, alphabetic poem. Psalm 112 is remarkably like Psalm 111. But, while Psalm 111 is a hymn of praise, Psalm 112 is a wisdom poem, pondering on the qualities of the just man. The qualities that are lauded in Yahweh by the poet of Psalm 111 are attributed to the just man in Psalm 112.

1 Halleluia.

How happy is the man who has reverence for
    Yahweh
2 and finds great delight in his commands!

His offspring will be numerous in the land:
the families of upright men will be blessed.

3 Wealth and riches are in his house
his generosity will always endure.

4 Light will dawn in the darkness for the upright,
a light that is just and merciful and kind.

5 The good man is kind and generous.
He disposes his affairs with right judgment.

6 He will never be made to fall.
The just man will be remembered forever.

7 No rumor of danger will cause him to fear.
His heart is steady, trusting in Yahweh.

8 His heart is firm, he is not afraid.
He is happy
knowing he will triumph over his enemies.

9 Open-handed he gives to the needy;
his generosity will endure forever.

10 The evil man will glare in his resentment;
he will grind his teeth and waste away.
The abode of the wicked will perish.

Psalm 113 (112)

Psalm 113 begins a section of the psalter (Psalms 113-118) known as the "Hallel psalms" or the "Egyptian Hallel", so called because of its use in connection with the feast of Passover. "Hallel" is a Hebrew word for "praise". This particular psalm was originally a piece used in the worship of Israel, but the exact location of the poem in the cult is uncertain. The assembly is called upon to render their praise to Yahweh because of his marvelous deeds in the past, especially for the mercy that he has shown to the helpless: those whose lot had reduced them to a death-like state (the lowly in the "dust", verse 7), the poor, and the sterile (a category of women whose lack of children classed them as being outside the blessings of the covenant).

1   Halleluia.

    Praise the works of Yahweh!
    Praise the name of Yahweh!

2   May the name of Yahweh be blest
    from now to eternity!

3   From the rising of the sun to its setting
    may the name of Yahweh be praised!

4   High above all nations is Yahweh,
    above the heavens, his glory!

5   Who is like Yahweh, our God—
    the One enthroned on high,

6   the One who bends down
    to look upon heaven and earth,

7   the One who raises the lowly from the dust?
    He lifts the poor from the heap of ashes

8   to seat them with princes, the very princes of his
      people.

9 The woman who is barren
   he makes a happy mother of children.

   Halleluia.

Psalm 114 (113a)

It is possible that Psalm 114 was born of a celebration in ancient Israel that commemorated the act of Yahweh taking possession of the land of Palestine. Certainly the poem describes this event in awe-inspiring terms: the land, originally pagan and secular, was made holy and even a sanctuary after the events of the exodus (verses 1-2). The mighty sea and the Jordan fled at his approach; the mountains and high places in the land, the cultic spots and the very residences of the pagan gods, quivered in terror as the Lord came unto his own (verses 3-6). Verses 7-8 renew the action of God in the liturgy and recall how he made the driest places yield fruitful water at his coming.

1 After Israel came out of Egypt,
   the house of Jacob from a people so barbaric,

2 Judah became the Lord's own holy place,
   and Israel his dominion.

3 The sea beheld it and ran away;
   the Jordan turned and ran back.

4 The mountains capered like startled rams,
   the high-places like the young sheep of the flock.

5 What was it, sea, that made you run away,
   Jordan, that you turned and ran back,

6 mountains, that you capered like startled rams,
   and you high-places,
   like the young sheep of the flock?

7 O Land, tremble now before the face of the
            Sovereign Lord,
   before the face of the God of Jacob,

8 who turned the rock into a pool of water,
   the flint into flowing fountains.

Psalm 115 (113b)

Scholars seem to be generally in agreement that Psalm 115 was originally a liturgical dialogue of some sort, and that the various parts of the poem were sung antiphonally by choirs answering one another. But it has been impossible to come to an agreement about which choir or group sang which parts of the psalm. The purpose of the whole psalm seems to be a hymn of encouragement in some time of trial. The poem begins (verses 1-2) almost like a national lament. Verses 3-8 form a sarcastic attack against the powerlessness of pagan idols. Verses 9-15 are a priestly blessing on the whole community. The psalm concludes with a brief hymn of praise (verses 16-18). Most authorities believe that Psalm 115 dates from a period after the Babylonian exile.

1   Not for our sake, Yahweh—not for us
    but for the sake of your name show your glory,
    because of your unfailing love and because of your
        faithfulness.

2   Why should the nations ask:
    "Where is their God?"

3   Our God is in heaven
    and he does whatever pleases him.

4   Their idols of silver and gold
    are the work of human hands.

5   They have mouths but do not speak
    and eyes but do not see.

6   They have ears but do not hear;
    they have noses but do not smell.

7   They have hands but do not feel
    and feet but do not walk.
    No sound ever comes from their throats at all.

8   Those who make them
    will become just like them,
    and so will everyone who puts his trust in them.

9   Israel, trust in Yahweh.
     He is their help and their protection.

10   House of Aaron, trust in Yahweh.
     He is their help and their protection.

11   You that reverence Yahweh,
     trust in Yahweh.
     He is their help and their protection.

12   Yahweh has remembered us—may he now bless
       us!
     May he bless the House of Israel.
     May he bless the House of Aaron.

13   May he bless those who reverence Yahweh,
     the lowly as well as the great.

14   May Yahweh increase you more and more—
     you and your children too.

15   May you be blessed by Yahweh,
     who made heaven and earth.

16   The heaven of heavens belongs to Yahweh,
     but he has given the earth to the children of men.

17   It is not the dead who praise Yahweh,
     not those who have gone down
     to the citadel of death.

18   But we will bless Yahweh;
     we will bless him from now to eternity.

Psalm 116 (114-115)

A song of thanksgiving for an individual. Some hold that the individual in question in this psalm was a public figure, even a king, but this cannot be determined with certainty. The poem opens with a description of the poet's situation (verses 1-6). Verses 7-15 are the psalmist's soliloquy concerning his deliverance. Veres 16-17 quote from the poet's prayer, and verses 18-19 return to the poet's inner dialogue.

1 Yahweh listened to me in his love;
   he heard my cry and my plea.

2 Yes, he inclined his ear toward me even as I was
   calling.

3 The bands of Death surrounded me;
   the delegations from Sheol caught up with me.

   I was overtaken by anguish and mourning,
4 but I called on the name of Yahweh:
   "I beg you, Yahweh, rescue my life!"

5 Yahweh is gracious and generous;
   our God is compassionate.

6 Yahweh is the guardian of the innocent:
   I had been brought low yet he saved me.

7 Be calm once more, my soul,
   because Yahweh has been generous in his gifts to
   you.

8 My soul, you have been rescued from Death;
   you, my eyes, from Tears,[a]
   and you, my feet, from Banishment.

9 So I will walk in the presence of Yahweh,
   in the presence of Yahweh in the Fields of Life.

---

a "Tears", "Banishment" and "Calamity" (verse 10) are poetic names for the Realm of Death.

10 I remained faithful even while I was being pursued
   and badgered by Calamity.

11 In my alarm I thought
   "No man is reliable!"

12 How can I ever repay Yahweh
   for all his generosity to me?

13 I will raise the cup of salvation.
   I will call on the name of Yahweh.

14 I will fulfill my vows to Yahweh
   in the very presence of all his people.

15 Precious in the eyes of Yahweh
   is the death of those who are devoted to him.

16 O Yahweh, I am truly your servant;
   indeed, I am your servant
   and your faithful child.
   Set me free from my bonds!

17 I will offer you a sacrifice of thanksgiving
   and I will call on your name, O Yahweh.

18 I will fulfill my vows to Yahweh
   in the presence of all his people,

19 in the court of the house of Yahweh,
   in the heart of Jerusalem.

Psalm 117 (116)

Because of its brevity and content, some scholars believe that this little poem was originally placed in its present position in the psalter as a conclusion to Psalm 116 or an introduction to Psalm 118. But this is unlikely; besides, if this is done the theological grandeur of this tiny poem is too readily over-looked. Psalm 117 bursts the bonds of a national narrowness and reveals the real heights and depths of the thought of ancient Israel: it calls on all the heathens to partake of the liturgical praise of Israel. Considering that this privilege of worshipping the Lord was of the very essence of what it meant to be an Israelite (cf. Exodus 3:18, 4:23), the call that this poem issues to the pagans to join in that worship is sublime indeed and recognized as such by Saint Paul in Romans 15:11.

1   Praise Yahweh, all nations!
     Acclaim him, all peoples!

2   His unfailing love toward us
     has been mighty
     and the faithfulness of Yahweh
     lasts until eternity.

     Halleluia.

Psalm 118 (117)

A psalm celebrating the victory of Yahweh and his king. It may be that the victory was not an actual military conflict, but the annual celebration at the new year of the Lord's victory over the forces of chaos and the renewal of the kingship of the monarchy of Israel. Many scholars believe that the king was annually deposed and then reinstated in his position, and this psalm may well celebrate such an occasion. Verses 1-4 call on all to join in the celebration of the triumph. The course of the "battle" and its outcome are described in verses 5-18, in which the intervention of Yahweh and his rescue of the king from death receive special attention. The triumphal procession and the rejoicing of both people and king are the subject of verses 19-29.

1   Thank Yahweh because he is good:
    his love is everlasting.

2   Let this be the theme of Israel's song:
    his love is everlasting.

3   Let this be the theme of the House of Aaron's
          song:
    his love is everlasting.

4   Let this be the theme of the song
    of those who reverence Yahweh:
    his love is everlasting.

5   I called to Yahweh
    from the narrowness where I was confined,
    and Yahweh himself answered me
    from the Vastness where he dwells.

6   Yahweh is on my side,
    so I am not afraid.
    What can man do to me?

7   Yahweh, my Mighty Warrior, is on my side,
    and so I will look in triumph on my enemies.

8 It is better to rely on Yahweh
  than to depend on man.

9 It is better to rely on Yahweh
  than to depend on princes.

10 All the nations were surrounding me,
   but in the name of Yahweh I cut them down.

11 They were surrounding me, yes, they were closing
       in on me,
   but in the name of Yahweh I cut them down.

12 They were swarming around me like bees
   and crackling like a fire among thorns,
   but in the name of Yahweh I cut them down.

13 You kept on pushing me until I almost fell,
   but Yahweh came to my help.

14 Yahweh was fortress and sentry for me
   and he became victory for me as well.

15 Cheers and cries of "Victory!"
   from the victor's tents!
   Yahweh's right hand brought the victory!

16 Yahweh's right hand was held high!
   Yahweh's right hand brought the victory!

17 I did not die but I lived
   so I could proclaim the deeds of Yahweh.

18 Though Yahweh punished me severely,
   he did not hand me over to death.

19 Open the gates of victory
   so I may go in to thank Yahweh.

20 This is the gate that belongs to Yahweh:
   let the victorious go in through it.

21 I thank you because you answered me
   and became my victory.

22 The stone that the builders rejected
has become the cornerstone.

23 This was Yahweh's doing
and it is marvelous for us to see.

24 This is the day of Yahweh's triumph,
a day for us to rejoice and be glad.

25 Yahweh, we beg you, grant victory!
Yahweh, we beg you, grant prosperity![a]

26 Blessed is he
who comes in the name of Yahweh!
We bless you in the house of Yahweh.

27 Yahweh God has indeed shown us his light!
Decorate the sanctuary with fronds of green[b]
and adorn the horns of the altar.

28 You are my God and I thank you;
my God, I praise you to the heavens!

29 Thank Yahweh because he is good:
his love is everlasting.

a This and the following verse were chanted by the crowds as Jesus trium-
phantly entered Jerusalem (cf. Mk 11:10).
b "Fronds of green": Jewish traditions link this psalm to the fall festival called
"Tabernacles". Part of the ceremonies of this feast called for the use of
branches generally thought to give concrete representation to the prayers of
the people for a fertile growing season in the months to come.

Psalm 119 (118)

Psalm 119, the longest poem in the collection of the psalms, is generally classified as a hymn in honor of the Law and of the Law-giver. It is a remarkable acrostic, with another acrostic concealed within the first. The principal acrostic device is the fact that the psalm consists of twenty-two strophes, each one consisting of eight verses and each verse within the strophe beginning with the same letter of the Hebrew alphabet. The other device is that eight names or synonyms for the Law are used in each strophe, with but three exceptions (verses 160, 168, and 172). It is believed that the number eight bore some special significance to the author. Perhaps it was regarded in his time as a symbol of perfection, being the completion of the number seven which was already thought of as an expression of wholeness. The psalm is powerfully expressive of a deep devotion to the Law and to the Lord. Every verse of this lengthy poem either speaks about God or to him. Some writers tend to dismiss this poem as little more than a kind of clever literary performance. But there is a depth of feeling and a vivacity of thought that is quite apparent to anyone who closely examines the psalm which makes it a fitting prayer for both Jews and Christians.

Psalm 119A—Aleph

1 How fortunate they are:
the men of blameless life,
the men who walk the way of Yahweh's law!

2 How fortunate are men who keep his rulings
and seek him with all their hearts!

3 They never do any wrong;
rather, they walk in his ways.

4 You yourself gave the order
that your directives are to be kept.

5 How I wish I were faithful,
in all my ways observing your decrees.

6 Then I would not be ashamed
when I contemplate all your commands.

7   I praise you with a heart that is honest,
    because I am learning your just decisions.

8   I will obey your decrees.
    Do not abandon me, O Great, O Eternal One.

Psalm 119B—Beth

9   How can a young man keep himself pure?
    By maintaining his paths according to your word.

10 I seek you with all my heart:
    do not let me stray from your commands.

11 I treasure your promise in my heart,
    so that I will not sin against you.

12 Praise to you, Yahweh!
    Teach me your decrees!

13 I recite them with my lips:
    all the decisions that come from your mouth.

14 Walking in the way of your rulings,
    I am overjoyed in you
    more than in all riches.

15 Let me ponder your directives;
    yes, let me contemplate your paths.

16 I am delighted by your decrees.
    I will never forget your words.

Psalm 119C—Gimel

17 Reward your servant:
    then will I live and keep your words.

18 Open my eyes,
    so I can contemplate the marvels of your law.

19 I am only an alien in the land:
    do not hide your commands from me.

20 My soul yearns;
   I long for your decisions at all times.

21 Rebuke the insolent,
   the accursed who have strayed from your
      commands.

22 Remove disgrace and shame from me,
   because I have obeyed your rulings.

23 Corrupt officials are taking their seats
   to judge me with foolish talk,
   but your servant ponders your decrees.

24 Yes, your rulings are my delight;
   they also counsel me.

Psalm 119D—Daleth

25 My soul lies flat in the mire of the world below;
   bring me back to life as you promised.

26 Because I told of your ways, you answered me;
   teach me your decrees.

27 Help me understand the ways of your directives,
   that I may ponder on your wonders.

28 My whole being droops in dejection.
   Lift me up as you promised.

29 Keep me far from the road of deceit.
   Show me your favor through your law.

30 I have chosen the way of truth:
   I hold your decisions in highest esteem.

31 I have clung to your rulings;
   O Lord, do not let me be put to shame.

32 I will run the way of your commands.
   Just increase my understanding!

Psalm 119E—He

33 Teach me, Yahweh, the way of your decrees.
I will guard it as my reward.

34 Give me understanding and I will keep your law.
I will observe it with all my heart.

35 Direct me on the path of your commands,
because that is where I have my delight.

36 Dispose my heart to prefer your rulings,
rather than unjust profit.

37 Make my eyes look away from idols.
Give me life under your dominion.

38 Honor the promise you made to your servant:
it is for those who reverence you.

39 Remove my disgrace, which causes me unrest,
because your decisions are beneficial.

40 Take note how I love your directives.
Give me life in your generosity!

Psalm 119F—Waw

41 O Yahweh, let your unfailing love overtake me:
the deliverance which you promised!

42 Let me have an answer for the one who baits me,
because I have faith in your word.

43 Do not take the true word away from my mouth,
O Great, O Eternal One.
How I have longed for your decisions!

44 Let me keep your law continually,
to eternity and beyond.

45 Let me walk with freedom,
while I seek your directives.

46 Let me announce your rulings
   in the presence of kings
   without ever being humiliated.

47 I will find my delight in your commands,
   because I love them.

48 I will lift my hands to your commands that I love;
   I will ponder on your decrees.

Psalm 119G—Zayin

49 Keep in mind the promise you made to your
         servant:
   you have given me reason to put my hope in it.

50 In my affliction this is what comforts me:
   that your word keeps me alive.

51 The scornful have treated me with abuse,
   O Great, O Eternal One;
   but I did not wander away from your law.

52 When I remember the decisions you made long
         ago,
   then, O Yahweh, I feel comforted.

53 Violent anger seizes me,
   because wicked men have abandoned your law.

54 Your decrees have become sentries for me
   in the house where I am a stranger.

55 At night I remember your name, O Yahweh;
   during its watches I remember your law.

56 I had to endure reproach,
   because I kept your directives.

Psalm 119H—Heth

57 O Yahweh, my Creator, I make this promise:
   I will keep your words!

58 I beg you with all my heart:
    have mercy on me according to your promise.

59 I reflected on your ways;
    I directed my steps back to your rulings.

60 I was prompt rather than remiss
    in keeping your commands.

61 The ropes of evil men enmeshed me,
    but I did not forget your law.

62 At midnight I rise from my rest
    to thank you for your generous decisions.

63 I have joined myself with all who reverence you,
    and with those who follow your directives.

64 The earth is filled
    with your unfailing love, O Yahweh.
    Teach me your decrees!

Psalm 119I—Teth

65 Be as kind to your servant, O Yahweh,
    as your words are kind.

66 Teach me how to judge and how to know,
    because I put faith in your decisions.

67 Before I was brought under discipline,
    I went astray;
    but now I keep your word.

68 You are the Kind One and you act with kindness.
    Teach me your decrees!

69 Scornful men brand me with lies,
    but I observe your directives with all my heart.

70 Their minds are dense and closed,
    but I have my delight in your law.

71 It was good for me to suffer hardship
   that I might learn your decrees.

72 Dearer to me than thousands of gold and silver
      coins:
   the law that issues from your mouth.

73 Your hands made me and fashioned me.
   Give me insight and I will learn your commands.

74 Those who reverence you will see me and be glad,
   because I wait for your promise.

75 I know, Yahweh, that your decisions are just:
   that it was out of faithfulness you humbled me.

76 Let your unfailing love act as my comfort,
   just as you promised me, your servant.

77 Let your compassion overtake me and I will live,
   because your law is my delight.

78 Let the scornful be humiliated,
   because they tried to corrupt me with a lie.
   But I pondered on your directives.

79 Let those who reverence you turn to me
   and they will acknowledge your rulings.

80 Let my heart be virtuous through your decrees,
   so I will not be disgraced.

81 My soul is pining away for your salvation;
   I wait for your promise.

82 My vision grows weak as I watch for your word.
   "When will it console me?"

83 Yes, I am like a man
who has tears brought to his eyes by smoke,
but I have not forgotten your decrees.

84 Just how many days does your servant have?
When will you carry out your decision
on those who persecute me?

85 The scornful have dug pits for me to fall into:
they do not live according to your law.

86 All your commands are faithful:
help me because they are persecuting me with lies!

87 They nearly obliterated me from the earth,
but I did not abandon your directives.

88 According to your unfailing love, give me life
and I will obey the rulings that come from your
    mouth.

Psalm 119L—Lamedh

89 Yahweh, your promise remains forever;
it is founded more firmly than the heavens.

90 Your faithfulness extends through every
        generation:
it will continue more solid than the very ground.

91 By your decision they still remain today,
because all things are your servants.

92 Had your law not been my delight,
I would have perished because of my hardships.

93 I will never forget your directives;
it is through them you give life to me.

94 I belong to you.
Save me, because I study your directives!

95 The wicked are just waiting to make an end of
        me,
    but I am trying to understand your rulings.

96 O Great God, I have never seen such perfection in
        anything
    as there is in the commands you give,
    O Final Destiny of us all.

Psalm 119M—Mem

97 How I love your law!
    I meditate on it all day long.

98 Your command makes me wiser than my foes,
    because it is with me always.

99 I have more insight than all my teachers,
    because I meditate on your rulings.

100 I have more understanding than old men,
    because I have followed your directives.

101 I have kept my feet from the path of evil,
    so that I may keep your word.

102 I do not turn away from your decisions,
    since you are the one who taught me.

103 How sweet your words are to my taste!
    They taste better than honey to me.

104 I gain insight from your directives,
    and so I loathe all deceptive paths.

Psalm 119N—Nun

105 Your word is a lamp for my feet
    and a light on my path.

106 I took an oath and I will adhere to it:
    I will keep your just decisions.

107 I am as despondent as those in the Realm of
    Doom.
    Yahweh, guard my life as you promised.

108 Delight me, Yahweh, with the words you speak.
    Teach me your decisions.

109 My life is in your everlasting hands,
    and so I do not forget your law.

110 Evil men have set a trap for me,
    but I do not wander away from your directives.

111 I have inherited your rules, O Eternal One,
    because they are the joy of my heart.

112 I set my heart on obeying your decrees.
    My reward will be eternal.

Psalm 119O—Samekh

113 I hate people who are lukewarm,
    but I love your law.

114 My Protector, my Suzerain, are you.
    I long for your promise.

115 Leave me, you evil men,
    and I will keep the commands of God.

116 Sustain me with your promise and I will live,
    but do not let me be disgraced because of my
    hope.

117 Give me support and I will be delivered,
    and I will always respect your decrees.

118 Expel everyone who strays from your decrees:
    their idolatry surely is a fraud.

119 All the wicked men of the land
    you discard like waste:
    that is why I love your decrees.

120   My flesh tingles with awe of you:
      I reverence your decisions.

Psalm 119P—Ayin

121   Execute a judgment for me which is just;
      do not leave me to those who malign me.

122   Make yourself the pledge of your servant's
          welfare:
      do not let the scornful oppress me.

123   My vision fails from looking for your deliverance
      and for your generous promise.

124   In dealing with your servant,
      show your unfailing love.
      Teach me your decrees.

125   I am your servant.
      Give me insight and I will comprehend your
          rulings!

126   Now is the time to take action, Yahweh;
      they have violated your law.

127   God, Most High and Truthful,
      I love your commands more than gold,
      even the finest gold.

128   God, Most High and Truthful,
      I accept all your directives as right.
      I loathe every way that leads to deceiving
          idolatry.

Psalm 119Q—Pe

129   God, Most High and Truthful,
      your rulings are marvelous:
      my soul keeps them.

130   Reveal your words which give light!
      Confer insight upon the uninstructed.

131   My mouth is open and my breathing is fast,
because I long for your commands.

132   Turn to me and have mercy on me,
just as you do for those who love your name.

133   Steady my steps with your promise;
let no idol have dominion over me.

134   Rid me of the oppressions that men cause,
and I will keep your directives.

135   Look kindly on your servant.
Teach me your decrees.

136   Torrents of tears are streaming from my eyes,
because men do not keep your law, O Most High.

Psalm 119R—Tsade

137   You are just, O Yahweh.
You are upright in your decisions.

138   You decreed your rulings justly:
faithfulness was the demand you made, O Great
God.

139   Jealous men were trying to exterminate me,
because my enemies forgot your word.

140   Your promise is fire-tested, O Great One.
How your servant loves it!

141   Even if I am young and scorned,
I have not forgotten your directives.

142   Your justice is generous, O Eternal One,
and your law is true.

143   Though hardship and trouble overtake me,
still your commands are my delight.

144   O Eternal One,
help me understand the justice of your rulings,
and I will live.

145 With all my heart I will call out.
Answer me, Yahweh, and I will observe your
decrees!

146 I called on you to save me.
I will surely obey your rulings.

147 I looked toward you at twilight and called for
help.
I waited for your words.

148 I looked toward you through the watches of the
night,
while I pondered on your promises.

149 In your unfailing love
listen to my voice, O Yahweh.
Give me life according to your decisions.

150 Idol-chasers approach:
they have left your law far behind.

151 But you are never far away, O Yahweh;
indeed, your commands agree with reality.

152 God of Eternity, I acknowledge your rulings;
before time began you decreed them.

Psalm 119T—Resh

153 Look at my hardships and set me free,
because I have not forgotten your law.

154 Plead my cause and redeem me.
Give me life according to your promise!

155 Keep wicked men away from your salvation,
because they do not study your decrees.

156 Your acts of compassion are many, O Yahweh.
Give me life according to your decisions!

157 My persecutors and adversaries are many,
but I do not turn from your rulings.

158 I looked at the devious and I was appalled,
because they have not held to your promises.

159 See how I love your directives!
O Yahweh, give me life in your unfailing love!

160 Truth is the essence of your word, O Eternal One;
the meaning behind your decisions is justice.

Psalm 119U—Sin

161 Corrupt officials harass me without cause,
and my heart was in great dread of my pursuers.

162 But I took joy from your promises,
like one who realizes an immense profit.

163 I hate and reject deceit,
but I love your law.

164 Seven times a day I praise you
for your generous decisions.

165 There is great peace
for those who love your law;
there is no tripping them up.

166 I hope for your salvation, O Yahweh,
while I obey your commands.

167 My soul keeps your rulings;
I have deep love for them.

168 I obey your directives and your rulings;
all my ways are in your presence.

Psalm 119V—Taw

169 Let my resounding cry come before you, Yahweh.
Give me insight as you promised.

170 Let my prayer come into your presence.
Deliver me according to your word!

171 Let my lips proclaim your praise,
because you have taught me your decrees.

172 Let my tongue repeat your words,
because all your commands are just.

173 Let your hand be there to help me,
because I have chosen your directives.

174 I long for your salvation, O Yahweh;
your law is my delight.

175 Let me live and I will praise you!
Let your decisions help me!

176 Should I wander like a stray sheep,
seek your servant,
because I have not forgotten your commands!

Psalm 120 (119)

Psalms 120 to 134 inclusive all bear the title "Song of Ascents". The meaning intended by him who bestowed this title on these 15 psalms has been the object of a long-standing quest by scholars. Many explanations have been offered; among them are the suggestions that these were songs sung by pilgrims on their ascent to Jerusalem, that these songs were sung by choirs on the stairs ("ascents") of the temple in Jerusalem, and that the word "ascents" refers to a literary device within the poems themselves, that is, the repetition and intensified use of a word in a verse that occurred in the verse immediately preceding. An example of this phenomenon would be the repetition of the words "deceitful tongue" in verses 2 and 3 of Psalm 120.

The classification of the present poem, Psalm 120, is problematical. Some think it is a personal lament while others see in it a kind of psalm of thanksgiving for a petition already answered. In verse 1 the psalmist proclaims the position of the poet who is still in danger. Perhaps he is a king who is assailed by rebellious vassals.

1   *A song of ascents.*

    To Yahweh I called when I was under attack
    and he answered me.

2   Yahweh, save my life from lying lips
    and from deceitful tongues.

3   You deceitful tongue, what will he give you?
    And what more will be given you besides?[a]

4   The sharpened arrows of a warrior
    and glowing coals of broom-wood.

---

[a] The two questions which the psalmist puts here are perhaps his answer to the oath taken by his opponent; there seems to have been a formula for an oath that would fit the bill here: "May Yahweh do such and such to me and add still more besides if . . . "

5   What misery is mine!
     My fate is the same whether I wander in
        Meshech[b]
     or live in the tents of Kedar.[c]

6   I would still be living too close,
     too close to men who hate peace.

7   I was in favor of peace
     and I said so;
     but they wanted only war.

[b] Meshech: a barbarous people of Asia Minor, whose name was sometimes used symbolically for enemies of God. Cf. Ezekiel 38 and 39.
[c] Kedar: an Arabian tribe of Bedouin.

Psalm 121 (120)

A psalm of blessing. The theme of the benedictions in this psalm is the protection bestowed by Yahweh on those who refrain from practicing idolatry and remain loyal to him. In verses 1 and 2 a leader, probably a priest, introduces the psalm with a liturgical queston and answer: Where would his protection come from if he were to look in suspense to the mountains where the idols were worshipped? His help is from Yahweh. Verses 3-8 pronounce the blessings on those who are faithful.

1   *A song of ascents.*

   If I raise my eyes to the mountains,
   where would my help come from?

2   My help comes from the presence of Yahweh,
   the One who made heaven and earth.

3   He will not let you lose your footing
   because your Guardian will not grow drowsy.

4   The Guardian of Israel does not sleep—
   nor will he ever slumber.[a]

5   Yahweh is your Guardian,
   Yahweh is your Shade as he stands at your side.

6   By day the sun will not strike you
   nor the moon by night.[b]

7   Yahweh will guard you from all evil:
   he will guard your life.

8   Yahweh will guard your going and your coming
   from now until eternity.

---

[a] The false gods, the Baals, "slept" during the dry season and needed awakening. Cf. 1 Kings 18:27.

[b] The dangers of sunstroke are known to ancients and moderns alike. But men of old thought that much harm came from being "moonstruck" as well.

Psalm 122 (121)

A song of pilgrimage to Jerusalem. This certainly is an unusual poem. Two things seem remarkable even at a cursory reading: the poet is at pains to give reasons for going to Jerusalem (verses 3-5) and then he pronounces blessings on the holy city (verses 6-9) and he seems compelled to legitimize those benedictions as well. It almost seems as if the psalmist were doing something that those around him generally frowned at. Perhaps he was a resident of the northern kingdom after the split of the monarchy who continued making pilgrimages to Jerusalem.

1   *A song of ascents of David.*

    I was glad with those who said to me:
    "We are going to the house of Yahweh."

2   Our feet will stand within your gates, O
        Jerusalem!

3   Jerusalem is a city built to be his;
    he planned it to be compact and secure.

4   To Jerusalem the tribes go up,
    the tribes of Yahweh.
    It is a solemn command, O Israel,
    to give thanks to the Name of Yahweh.

5   In Jerusalem is the throne of judgment,
    the throne of the house of David.

6   May they pray for your peace, Jerusalem;
    those who love you—may they prosper!

7   May there be peace within your walls;
    may there be prosperity within your towers.

8   For the sake of my brothers and my friends
    I say sincerely: "Peace be within you!"

9   For the sake of the house of Yahweh, our God,
    I will pray for what is good for you.

Psalm 123 (122)

A lament of the nation. An official speaker prays in the name
of the group in this moving prayer for release from the scorn of
faithless men. In verses 1 and 2 the psalmist compares the
suspense-filled vigil of himself and of his nation to the attitude
of slaves watching the hand of the master till he gives the sign
to issue blessings. Verses 3 and 4 make a plea for divine favor
because the community suffers under the load of disdain
heaped on them by unidentified enemies. These may be idolaters, Israelite or foreign, who laugh at the attempts of the
pious to be faithful to the law when so many opportunities are
available to the lawless. However, the identity of these persons
must remain conjectural.

1 *A song of ascents.*

Toward you I have turned my eyes,
toward heaven where you are enthroned.

2 As the eyes of servants follow their master's hand,
and the eyes of a maid, the hand of her mistress,
so we keep our eyes on Yahweh, our God,
until he has mercy on us.

3 Have mercy on us, Yahweh!
Have mercy on us!
How heavily does contempt weigh us down!

4 Our souls have had more than enough scorn
from the carefree
and insults from the proud.

Psalm 124 (123)

A song of national thanksgiving. No precise occasion can be assigned for the use of this little song in the Old Testament. It is not unlikely that it was sung during some great festival. The cause of the thanksgiving was that it was Yahweh who rescued Israel from peril, and if it had not been Yahweh, the deliverance would not have been accomplished. The images of the danger that had threatened are images that were generally associated with the nether-world: the yawning abyss waiting to consume all men (verse 3), the raging waters of the chaos (verses 4-5) and the stealthy hunter (verse 7). Thus Yahweh has power even against the puissant forces of Death.

1   *A song of ascents of David.*

    Were it not that Yahweh was for us—
    well might Israel say it—

2   were it not that Yahweh was for us,
    the men who attacked us would have swallowed us
        alive,

3   while their anger raged against us.

4   A torrent of water would have flooded us,
    cresting above our necks;

5   the rampaging waters would have crested
        over our heads.

6   Praise Yahweh!
    He did not let us fall victim to their teeth.

7   Like a bird, our necks have escaped
    from the noose of the fowler.
    The noose is broken
    and we have escaped.

8   Our help is in the Name of Yahweh,
    the One who made heaven and earth.

Psalm 125 (124)

There is no general agreement among scholars as to the exact genre into which Psalm 125 ought to be categorized. It seems to be a prophetic piece, possibly used for a new year liturgy. Verses 1-2 are an expression of confidence that those who trust in Yahweh will be as firm as Zion itself. Since Zion was regarded as the earthly dwelling of the Lord such a statement inspired unbounded reliance. Verse 3 lays down the condition for divine protection: fidelity on the part of Jerusalem. The "wicked" mentioned in this verse are doubtless some foreign enemies. Verse 4 prays for blessings and verse 5 contains a mild imprecation on the unfaithful.

1   *A song of ascents.*

    Those who put their trust in Yahweh
    are like the Mountain of Zion:

2   the One enthroned in Jerusalem
    will never be overthrown.

    As mountains surround her,
    Yahweh surrounds his people
    from now until eternity.

3   The scepter of the wicked will surely not rest
    over the land allotted to the just,
    as long as the just
    will not reach out their hands to idols.

4   Show goodness to the good, O Yahweh,
    and to the upright of heart.

5   But as for those who waver on devious paths,
    may Yahweh make them vanish with idolaters.
    Peace upon Israel!

Psalm 126 (125)

A national thanksgiving to be used at the autumnal festival. This hymn celebrates the joy of a good growing season and harvest (verses 1-3) and recalls the promises made to the patriarchs (Genesis 22:17). Verses 4-6 already contemplate the coming year and pray for an abundant crop harvested after the hardships of planting and growing.

1   A song of ascents.

When Yahweh gives a good harvest time[a] to Zion
we become like the sands of the sea.

2   Then our mouths are filled with laughter
and shouts of joy are on our tongues.
Then even the nations say:
"Yahweh shows his greatness
as he works among them."

3   Yahweh does show his greatness
as he works among us!
How happy he has made us!

4   Give us, Yahweh, a good harvest time,
as abundant as the creeks become in the Negeb.[b]

5   May those who scatter their seeds in tears
reap their harvest with shouts of joy!

6   The man who goes out weeping
as he carries his sack of seed—
may he come back with a joyful shout,
carrying his sheaves of grain!

[a] The words "harvest time" are an attempt to translate a Hebrew expression that probably refers to the whole annual cycle of growing and harvesting crops.
[b] "Negeb": a region of southern Palestine, made fruitful in the winter because of rainfall, and otherwise only by irrigation.

Psalm 127 (126)

A psalm of uncertain genre. This poem has elements of a wisdom poem, but it appears to have been composed for the festival of tabernacles in the fall. Two themes connected with that festival appear in the psalm: the rededication of the temple and fertility. Verse 1 is an epigrammatic saying or perhaps two sayings about the temple and the city. Verses 2-5 are sayings about the fertility of the land and of people. The theme that underlies this psalm is that Yahweh is builder of city and temple, and giver of fertility to the soil and to men. The implication of this brief psalm seems to be a warning to be faithful to the Lord and not to go after the heathen idols.

1   *A song of ascents of Solomon.*

> If Yahweh does not build the temple
> in vain is the toil of those who build it.
> If Yahweh does not guard the city,
> in vain is the watching of him who guards it.

2   It is in vain that you rise early
> and stay up late at night,
> working for bread that idols give.
> God who is trustworthy prospers those he loves.

3   Sons are the inheritance Yahweh gives;
> the fruit of the womb, the reward he offers.

4   Like arrows in a warrior's hand
> are the sons of one's youth.

5   Happy the man
> who has filled his quiver with them!
> He will not be disgraced
> but will thrust his enemies back from the gate!

Psalm 128 (127)

Like its two predecessors, Psalms 126 and 127, this psalm is
very probably derived from the autumn feast. Though the
psalm resembles a wisdom psalm in verses 1-4, the last two
verses are reminiscent of a priestly blessing. The theme of this
poem is that Yahweh will prosper those who are faithful to
him. Verses 1-4 depict the domestic bliss and material prosperity of him who reverences the Lord, while the last two verses
form the words of a benediction pronounced over such a
devout person.

1 *A song of ascents.*

   How happy is every man who reverences
      Yahweh—
   everyone who walks in his ways!

2 You will eat the fruit of your own labors;
   happiness and blessing will be yours.

3 Your wife will be like a productive vine in your
      home,
   and your children like olive-seedlings around
      your table.

4 This is the way of Yahweh, who is trustworthy.
   He blesses the man who reverences him.

5 May Yahweh of Zion bless you!
   May you see the prosperity of Jerusalem
   all the days of your life!

6 May you see your children's children!
   Peace upon Israel!

Psalm 129 (128)

Psalm 129 appears to be a national lament, though not all commentators agree on the exact genre. Verses 1-4 describe in a poignant way the sufferings of the nation throughout its history. Verses 5-8 are a prayer for the defeat of Zion's enemies. The enemies of which this psalm speaks are unidentified. It is known that the Assyrians used to harrow the backs of defeated peoples, but the references in this psalm may be metaphorical.

1 *A song of ascents.*

Relentlessly they have oppressed me
ever since I was young—
well might Israel say it.

2 Relentlessly they have oppressed me
ever since I was young,
but never have they subdued me.

3 The plowmen have plowed on my back
and made long furrows on it.

4 May Yahweh, the Just One,
splinter the yoke of the wicked!

5 May all who hate Zion
be humiliated and forced to retreat!

6 May they be like grass on the roof,[a]
which withers away before the haying:

7 The reaper cannot fill his hands with it,
nor can the binder of the sheaves fill his sack.

---

a "Grass on the roof": Palestinian houses had flat roofs and on these was often a layer of dirt. But as this soil was thin, what grew in it dried up before it matured.

8 Those who pass by will be unable to say:
"Yahweh's blessing be yours!
We bless you in the name of Yahweh!"[b]

---

[b] The last words of verse 8 resemble a greeting shouted to harvesters of grain
as in Ruth 2:4.

Psalm 130

Numbered as the sixth among the penitential psalms, this poem is generally classified as an individual lament. But the speaker is apparently a leader who speaks for the nation and there is reason to believe that he is the king and that the psalm is a royal lament. Verses 1-6 are spoken in the first person. The poet cries from his misery as from the world of the dead ("the depths" is a name for Sheol). Aware that he (and his people) are guilty of sin, the psalmist compares his suspenseful wait for the Lord's mercy to the lonely vigil of guards in the night. Verses 7-8 call on Israel to wait for the Lord's generous forgiveness.

1   *A song of ascents.*

    Out of the depths I call to you, Yahweh;

2   O my Sovereign, hear my voice.
    Be attentive as I call for mercy.

3   O Yahweh, if you were to keep an account of
        guilt,
    who could survive, O my Sovereign?

4   But you are forgiving and worthy of reverence.

5   I call to Yahweh—with fervor I call
    and I am longing for his reply.

6   I wait for my Sovereign
    through the watches of the night—
    through all the watches of the night.

7   O Israel, wait for Yahweh
    because Yahweh's love never fails.

8   The ransom he provides is generous.
    Yes, he will ransom Israel from all her guilt.

Psalm 131 (130)

A psalm of innocence. The speaker in this poem is probably a king. It is not entirely clear of just which kind of arrogance the poet declares himself guiltless, but very possibly it is idolatry to which reference is made in verse 1. Verse 2 declares that the poet is firmly committed to trust in Yahweh while the last verse calls on the nation to join in this confidence. This last line is reminiscent of the last verse of Psalm 130.

1 *A song of ascents of David.*

O Yahweh, my heart is not arrogant,
nor are my eyes raised too high.

I am not engaged in things too great,
nor do I strive for things too wonderful for me.

2 I keep my soul calm and quiet,
like an infant with its mother;
with the Lord, my soul is like an infant.

3 O Israel, wait for Yahweh,
from now till eternity.

Psalm 132 (131)

A poem for the liturgy of the renewal in the fall festival. This ancient poem commemorates the bringing of the Ark of the Covenant to Jerusalem by King David (2 Samuel 5-6). It is not unlikely that this poem formed the background of a procession with the Ark at this celebration. Verses 1-5 recall the devotion of David in his day which led to the solemn transport of the Ark. Verses 6-8 seem to be acclamations used in the procession. Verses 9-10 pray for the priests, the faithful and the king. Verses 11-18 recall the promises made by Yahweh to David and his realm.

1   *A song of ascents.*

    O Yahweh, remember David
    and all the effort he made—

2   how he swore to Yahweh,
    how he made this vow to the Mighty One of
        Jacob:

3   "I will not go under the canopy in my house,
    I will not lie down in the bed prepared for me.

4   I will not allow myself to sleep
    nor will I give repose to my eyes,

5   until I find a shrine for Yahweh—
    a dwelling for the Mighty One of Jacob."

6   We heard about this at Ephrathah[a]—
    we learned of it at the fields of Jaar.[b]

7   Let us go to his dwelling
    and bow down before the cushion of his feet.

---

[a] Ephrathah: another name for Bethlehem, the city of David.
[b] "Fields of Jaar": the place where the Ark had been kept before its removal to Jerusalem.

8 Rise up, Yahweh, and come to your
      resting-place—
  you and the Ark, your fortress.

9 May your priests be vested with justice
  and your devoted people sing for joy.

10 For the sake of David, your servant,
  do not reject the petition of your anointed king.

11 Yahweh swore this oath to David;
  surely he will never break it:
  "Upon your throne I shall place a son of yours.

12 And if your sons keep the covenant with me
  as well as the decrees that I teach them,
  their sons too will sit on your throne forever
      and ever."

13 This is because Yahweh has chosen Zion;
  he wants it as his dwelling:

14 "This is my resting-place forever;
  here I shall sit enthroned
  because I have chosen it.

15 I shall richly bless her pilgrims
  and I shall satisfy her poor with food.

16 I shall vest her priests with salvation
  and her devoted people will sing out for joy.

17 I shall make the strength of David glow
  and I shall trim a lamp for my anointed king.

18 I shall dress her foes in disgrace,
  but on his head will be a gleaming crown."

Psalm 133 (132)

Though one of the briefest poems in the psalter, Psalm 133 nonetheless does not readily yield the fullness of its meaning. It is usually classified as a wisdom psalm by scholars. The burden of the three verses that make up this poem is that great blessings of life and fertility will flow if the brethren of Israel worship together. The words "worship in unity" in verse 1 are generally translated as "live together"; but it is likely that the reference in this phrase is to the common celebration of the autumn feast. Possibly the poem originally was a wisdom piece to encourage unity in Israel, perhaps after the monarchy had divided. The brethren of the northern and southern kingdoms are here called upon, if this theory has any validity, to celebrate the feast of tabernacles together in Jerusalem.

1   *A song of ascents of David.*

What blessings, what joys there are
when brothers worship in unity!

2   It is like precious oil on the head,
running down onto the beard, onto Aaron's
     beard,
running down even to the hem of his robe.[a]

3   It is like the dew of Hermon[b]
that drops down to the mountains of Zion.
Life forever and ever is the blessing
that Yahweh bestows there.

---

a The anointing of Aaron is reported in Leviticus 8, but the significance of the abundance of the oil described here is mysterious though possibly suggestive of lavish fertility; cf. Gen. 27:28.

b Hermon: a perpetually snow-capped peak in the Anti-Lebanon mountain range in the north of Palestine. The surrounding areas are remarkable for the wetness of their dewfall. The phrase "dew of Hermon" probably is a proverbial expression for a very heavy dew.

Psalm 134 (133)

A brief liturgical hymn. Verses 1-2 are a call to praise, addressed to those who "stand in the house of Yahweh". Some feasts, particularly the feast of tabernacles, may have had nocturnal festivities. Verse 3 is in the form of a priestly blessing.

1 *A song of ascents.*

Come, praise the name of Yahweh,
you that stand in the house of Yahweh.

Come, praise the works of Yahweh
through all the watches of the night.ª

2 Lift your hands up to the holy place
and proclaim the praises of Yahweh.

3 And may Yahweh of Zion bless you—
Yahweh, who made both heaven and earth.

ª The wording of the translation of this verse has been freely rearranged to produce a more euphonic arrangement in English without essentially altering the sense of the Hebrew.

Psalm 135 (134)

A hymn of praise, the make-up of which owes much to other psalms. This poem was probably compiled as a hymn for the feast of Passover. It begins and ends with a call to praise (verses 1-3 and 19-21). Verses 4-7 acknowledge the greatness of the Lord in choosing Israel and in ruling over nature. Verses 8-14 recall the exodus and the divine providence in maintaining the chosen people. Verses 15-18 are a classical denunciation of the powerless idols to which other peoples look in vain for assistance.

1   Halleluia.

> Praise the name of Yahweh;
> praise the works of Yahweh,

2   you that stand in the house of Yahweh,
in the court of the house of our God.

3   Praise Yahweh!
How good Yahweh is!
How wonderful it is to sing hymns to his name!

4   Yahweh chose Jacob for himself
and Israel as his own treasured possession.

5   Yes, I acknowledge that Yahweh is great
and that our Sovereign is greater than all gods.

6   Yahweh has done whatever he pleases,
in heaven and on earth,
in the seas and the oceans deeps.

7   From the edge of the earth he brings up clouds;
he makes lightning for the rain
and leads the winds out of his storehouses.

8   He struck down the firstborn of Egypt,
of animals as well as man.

9   He sent signs and wonders into Egypt
against Pharaoh and all his slaves.

10 He struck down mighty nations
   and killed powerful kings—

11 King Sihon of the Amorites
   and King Og of Bashan,
   and all the kings of Canaan.

12 Then he presented their land to Israel—
   to his people as their estate.

13 Yahweh, that name of yours is eternal!
   Yahweh, that glorious title of yours will endure
         for all generations!

14 Yes, because Yahweh keeps his people safe
   and he is compassionate with all his servants.

15 But the idols of the nations are of silver and
         gold—
   the products of human hands.

16 They have mouths but do not speak
   and eyes but do not see;

17 they have ears but do not hear
   and there is not even breath in their mouths.

18 Those who make them
   and everyone who puts his trust in them—
   may they all become just like them.

19 House of Israel, bless Yahweh!
   House of Aaron, bless Yahweh!

20 House of Levi, bless Yahweh!
   You that reverence Yahweh, bless Yahweh!

21 Blest be Yahweh of Zion,
   the One who dwells in Jerusalem!

   Halleluia.

Psalm 136 (135)

A hymn of praise in the form of a litany. Among the Jews this psalm is known as "the Great Hallel", and tradition places it in the liturgy for the feast of Passover. The logical progression of the psalm is quite evident: verses 1-3 form a kind of exordium; verses 4-9 extol the wisdom of Yahweh and his power in creating the universe. The deliverance at the time of the exodus is the theme of verses 10-25. Verse 26 brings the song of praise to a grand conclusion.

1 Thank Yahweh! How good he is!
His love is everlasting!

2 Thank the God of gods!
His love is everlasting!

3 Thank the Lord of lords!
His love is everlasting!

4 He alone does wonderful deeds.
His love is everlasting!

5 In wisdom he made the heavens.
His love is everlasting!

6 He spread the earth over the waters.
His love is everlasting!

7 He made the great lights.
His love is everlasting!

8 The sun to rule over the day.
His love is everlasting!

9 The moon and stars to rule over the night.
His love is everlasting!

10 He struck down the firstborn of Egypt.
His love is everlasting!

11 He brought Israel out from that land.
His love is everlasting!

12 With strong hand and arm upraised he led them.
His love is everlasting!

13 He divided the Sea of Reeds.
His love is everlasting!

14 Through it he led Israel.
His love is everlasting!

15 But he evaded Pharaoh and all his army in the
Sea.
His love is everlasting!

16 He led his people across the desert.
His love is everlasting!

17 He struck down mighty kingdoms.
His love is everlasting!

18 He killed illustrious kings.
His love is everlasting!

19 King Sihon of the Amorites.
His love is everlasting!

20 And King Og of Bashan.
His love is everlasting!

21 He made their land an estate.
His love is everlasting!

22 It became an estate of his servant Israel.
His love is everlasting!

23 When we were cast down, he remembered us.
His love is everlasting!

24 He rescued us from our oppressors.
His love is everlasting!

25 He gives food to all living things.
His love is everlasting!

26 Thank the God of heaven!
His love is everlasting!

Psalm 137 (136)

A psalm of communal lamenting. It may well have been used on an annual day of mourning to commemmorate the fall of the city of Jerusalem at the time of the Babylonian exile. Verses 1-6 recall the bitter days of the exile when the Jews were subjected to taunts and jeers from their Babylonian captors. They remained unswervingly loyal and remembered Zion with immovable and even fierce affection. Verses 7-9 call down imprecations on the Edomites, former vassals of Jerusalem and related to the Jews by blood, and even stronger curses on the Babylonians, the destroyers of Jerusalem. These last verses of the psalm can only be correctly adjudged when considered against the backdrop of the ancient Near East. They are expressive of the feelings of poet and people toward their native land as much as of a helpless rage against those who invaded and plundered them.

1 On the banks of the rivers of Babylon
   we sat wailing,
   as we remembered Zion.

2 We left our harps hanging
   there on the poplar trees,

3 because our captors required the lyrics of a song
           from us—
   our tormentors, a happy tune.
   They said: "Sing us a song of Zion!"

4 How could we sing the song of Yahweh
   on foreign soil?

5 If I forget you, Jerusalem,
   let my right hand wither!

6 Let my tongue stick in my mouth
   if I do not remember you—

   if I do not wear you upon my head, Jerusalem,
   like a crown on a day of festivities.

7 O Yahweh, remember what the sons of Edom
said at the time Jerusalem was condemned:
"Shame her, shame her,
down to her very foundation!"

8 O Babylon, you plunder-loving city,
how blest will be the man
who pays you back in full
for the treatment you meted out to us!

9 How blest the man
who seizes your infants
and dashes them against a rock!

Psalm 138 (137)

A royal song of thanksgiving. Originally this may have been a
song of gratitude after an Israelite king had won a military
victory, but its original setting cannot be so precisely determined with certainty. The first three verses praise God for
what he has accomplished. Verses 4-5 predict the amazement
of foreign rulers at the news of Yahweh's deliverance of his
chosen king. Verses 6-8 close the poem with a prayer for future
protection in which the psalmist trusts because he is aware of
Yahweh's providence.

1   *Of David.*

    I will thank you with all my heart;
    before the gods I will sing hymns to you.

2   I will bow down toward your holy temple,
    in thanks I will praise your Name.

    In your unfailing love and your faithfulness
    you have glorified your Name and your promise
        before all men.

3   On the day I called, you gave me victory;
    you gave me courage and a feeling of strength.

4   All the kings of earth will praise you, Yahweh,
    when they hear the words you speak.

5   Of the dominion of Yahweh, they will sing:
    "How great is the glory of Yahweh!"

6   Although Yahweh is lofty,
    still he sees the lowly;
    although he is on high,
    he knows what is far away.

7   If I walk where my adversaries are around me,
    keep me alive while they rage against me!
    Stretch out your left hand
    and give me victory with your right hand.

8   May Yahweh avenge me as long as I live.
Yahweh, your unfailing love lasts forever.
Do not abandon the work of your own hands.

Psalm 139 (138)

The contents of this beautiful psalm seem relatively clear but
the exact designation of a genre that would adequately express
in a single phrase what these contents are has not yet been
found. Perhaps it would be best to describe Psalm 139 tenta-
tively as a "psalm of innocence". The speaker in this poem is
evidently a leader, possibly a king. He protests his innocence of
idolatry, and prays to be delivered from his accusers. That the
whole poem is a unified piece is illustrated by the similarity of
ideas in verses 1 and 23-24. In Verses 1-18 the psalmist prays
to God, confessing that all his actions are open to the divine
scrutiny. He begins by asking an examination to be conducted
by Yahweh himself. Verses 18-22 describe the poet's opponents
who are devoted to heathen idols, and he prays to be delivered
from them. In the final verses the psalmist again prays to be
judged only at the divine assizes.

1   *For the director: a psalm of David.*

    O Yahweh, examine me
    and then you will understand,

2   because you know when I sit down and stand up;
    you comprehend my thoughts even from a
        distance.

3   You appraise me as I leave and as I arrive
    and you govern all my travels.

4   A word is not even off my tongue
    and already you know all about it, Yahweh.

5   From the back and from the front,
    you close in on me
    and lay the palms of your hands upon me.

6   Your knowledge is too overwhelming for me;
    it soars too high, I cannot comprehend it.

7   Where could I get away from your spirit
    or where could I escape from your presence?

8 If I climb to the heavens, there you are,
and if I lie down in Sheol, you are there.

9 If I spread my wings in the east
to settle at the westernmost ocean,

10 even there your left hand would guide me,
your right hand would take hold of me.

11 Yes, I think he observes me even in the dark;
even in the night, there is light all around me.

12 The very darkness is not dark for you;
night shines for you as bright as the day—
for you, darkness is the same as light!

13 You are the One who created my innermost being;
you have sheltered me
since I was in my mother's womb.

14 I thank you, O Most High,
because you fill me with awe.
You are wonderful in your deeds,
and I kneel before you.

From of old you have known my very soul;
15 not even my bones have ever been concealed
from you.

Since the time I was molded in the hidden place,
kneaded together in the depths of the world
below,

16 your eyes have followed all the stages of my life,
and all of them have been entered in your book.

All my days had been fashioned,
though not a single one of them yet had passed.

17 For me how deep are your thoughts;
O God, how vast is the sum of them!

18   More numerous, were I to count them,
     than the grains of sand.
     I hope to awake and be with you always!

19   If only you would do away with the wicked, O
       God!
     If only the men who rely on idols
     would stay away from me!

20   They speak to every figurine
     and raise their eyes to rows of nothingness.

21   Do I not hate those who hate you, O Yahweh?
     Am I not appalled at those who challenge you?

22   I have rejected them entirely—
     they have become my enemies.

23   Examine me and understand my heart;
     test me and know my inner trials.

24   See if any idol has subjected me,
     and then lead me into the realm of eternity.

Psalm 140 (139)

An individual lament. The speaker in the psalm is apparently a king, but the situation of the poet is not easily determined. Some scholars have considered him to have been accused of some crime. Whatever his plight, he maintains unswerving fidelity to Yahweh throughout the psalm. Verses 14-15 declare the psalmist's conviction that Yahweh will definitely take action on his behalf and that all the righteous will have cause to rejoice.

1 *For the director: a psalm of David.*

2 Rescue me, Yahweh, from the evil man;
    from the man of violence, protect me:

3 they are plotting evil in their hearts
    and planning aggression all the day long.

4 They sharpen their tongues like the snake's,
    with the venom of serpents on their lips.

5 Guard me, Yahweh,
    from the hands of the wicked man;
    from the man of violence, protect me,
    because they are plotting to trip my feet.

6 The arrogant are hiding a snare for me
    and scoundrels are spreading a net.
    Beside the path they are putting out bait for me.

7 I make this declaration:
    "O Yahweh,
    you are my God!"
    O Yahweh, listen to my cry for mercy.

8 O Yahweh, my Sovereign Lord, my Fortress of
        salvation,
    shield my head on the day of conflict.

9 O Yahweh, do not give the evil man what he
        wants;
    do not promote his evil schemes, O Exalted One.

10 Those who plague me are all around me:
   may they be drowned in the venom of their own
      lips.

11 May he heap glowing coals upon them
   and hurl them into the Fire;
   let them not rise from the muddy Pit.

12 May the man who defames
   have no lasting home in the Land.
   May the man who lives by violence
   be hounded to ruin by deadly evil.

13 I know that Yahweh will intervene
   in the cause of the needy
   and for the rights of the poor.

14 The just will thank your Name;
   the upright will dwell before your face.

Psalm 141 (140)

An individual lament. The psalmist, in a spirit reminiscent of that of Elijah, prays to be delivered from the pressures and persecutions that idolaters put on him to join in their pagan worship. Verses 1-2 introduce the psalm: the psalmist's pure prayer is to serve for his sacrifice in a time when the official worship is too corrupt for him to partake in (cf. 1 Kings 18:36). Verses 4-7 form a prayer for deliverance from the wiles and the worship of those who engage in idolatry. In verse 5 the psalmist promises that no enticement or punishment will induce him to join these wretched men. Verses 6-7 are an imprecation on the leaders of these evil men: they are to fall into the hands of the "Rock", i.e., Yahweh, and be cast into the nether-world. There they will be soundly trounced; the comforting "words" of verse 6 are pure irony. Verses 8-10 conclude the poem with a final petition for deliverance. Very probably this psalm was a product of the northern kingdom, perhaps from the age of Elijah or afterward.

1   *A psalm of David.*

    Yahweh, I am calling for you.
    Come quickly to me.
    Listen to my cry as I call to you.

2   Let my prayer arise
    like incense before you;
    like the evening sacrifice
    be the raising of my hands.

3   Place a guard over my mouth;
    keep watch over the door of my lips.

4   Do not let a lying promise entice my heart;
    do not let me join in the infamous deeds
    of men who worship idols.
    May I never dine at their carousings!

5   Though the Just One strikes me,
    though the Kind One rebukes me,
    and the anointing oil never touches my head,
    my prayer will always be against the evil they do.

[313]

6   May their rulers blunder into the hands of the
        Rock
    and hear his words!
    Surely those words will comfort them!

7   He is like one splitting and chopping
    in the world below.
    "Our bones are scattered at the brink of Sheol."

8   But Yahweh, my Sovereign,
    I turn my eyes to you;
    I have trusted in you;
    do not leave me undefended.

9   Keep me out of range of the trap
    they have set for me,
    and from the allurements
    that idol-worshippers employ.

10   Let all those evil men fall into their own nets,
    while I alone bypass them.

Psalm 142 (141)

An individual lament. The circumstances under which this poem was composed and in which it was used cannot be determined. The psalmist sees himself in a situation which is like that of a man facing death (verses 2-4a). He is alone in his trying experience except for the help of Yahweh, for which he earnestly begs (verses 4b-8). In verse 7 he sees himself as the quarry in a hunt, and in verse 8 he has altered the metaphor and calls out from his prison. The dominant note of this poem is that Yahweh alone will be the salvation of the poet, and in this spirit it can be prayed today.

1   *A maskil of David. A prayer when he was in the cave.*

2   I call out to Yahweh for help;
    I plead aloud with Yahweh for mercy.

3   I pour my prayer out before him
    and in his presence I tell about my anguish.

4   My life's breath is ebbing away
    and you well know the path I am traveling.
    In the way that I must walk
    they have set a trap for me.

5   Just look on my right and you will see
    that there is no one at all who cares about me.
    All escape has fled from me
    because no one has any interest in me.

6   I call out to you, Yahweh, for help;
    I say: "You are my Refuge,
    my Inheritance in the land of life."

7   Listen closely to my cry—
    I am in the deepest sorrow.
    Save me from those who are hunting me down—
    they are far too strong for me.

8 Lead me out of this prison
so I can praise your name.
Let the just assemble around me
for you give generous rewards, O Most High.

Psalm 143 (142)

An individual lament. The psalmist appears to be a king in desperate straits. The dominant note throughout this piece is its urgency: the poet is near death (verses 3, 7, 10). But throughout he also maintains his confidence that Yahweh can and will rescue him. Psalm 143 is the last of the seven penitential psalms.

1 *A psalm of David.*

Hear my prayer, Yahweh;
O God, listen closely to my plea for mercy.
Answer me, because you are faithful and generous.

2 But do not go to court with your servant,
because no one alive
can stand acquitted before you.

3 How the Enemy is after me,
beating my life down to the world below!
He is driving me back into the place of darkness
like men who have died long ago.

4 My spirits are low;
my heart aches and is desolate.

5 I remember the days long past.
I ponder on all your deeds,
and meditate on all your hands have done.

6 I raise my hands up to you,
because like dry ground I thirst for you.

7 Come quickly to answer me, Yahweh,
because my breath is failing.
Do not hide your face from me,
or I will become like those
who go down into the Pit.

8 Let me hear of your kindness at dawn,
because I have trusted in you.
Guide me to the way I am to walk,
because I am waiting in suspense before you.

9 Deliver me from my enemies, Yahweh,
because I have secluded myself with you.

10 Teach me to do your will,
because you are my God.
Lead me by your good spirit
into the level land.[a]

11 For the sake of your Name, Yahweh,
give me life;
in your generosity,
lead me out of my anguish.

12 In your unfailing love,
exterminate my enemies;
bring all my adversaries to destruction,
because I am your servant.

a "The level land": the land of life, as opposed to the nether-world, the land of
death.

Psalm 144 (143)

Psalm 144 has become notorious among exegetes as being defiant of all attempts to categorize it. This is not because no literary category can be found for it but because the poem bears the marks of too many literary categories. The best explanation seems to be that it is a royal psalm, the prayer of a king for himself and his people. The seeming dependence of the psalm on other psalms is perhaps to be clarified most plausibly by saying that many of the phrases within the piece are taken from liturgical traditions on which other psalms also drew. In verses 1-11 the king, a descendant of David, prays for protection against his assailants and promises praise to Yahweh. The last four verses are a graphic prayer for the material well-being of his people. The rural character of this prayer seems to indicate a time of composition when the city of Jerusalem had not yet attained its central position as completely as it had by the date of the exile to Babylon.

1 *Of David.*

Praise to Yahweh, my Mountain!
He trains my hands for combat
and my arms for battle.

2 He is my Rampart and my Fortress,
my Bulwark and my Refuge.
He is the Shield I trust in,
who puts people under my feet.

3 Yahweh, what is man
that you should take note of him,
the son of man that you should have regard for
him?

4 Man is like a wisp of fog,
his days like a fleeting shadow.

5 Yahweh, lower your heavens and come down;
touch the mountains and they will give off smoke.

6 Flash your lightning and scatter the enemy;
forge your arrows and rout them.

7   Extend your hands from above
    to deliver me and rescue me from the deep waters.

    Save me from the hands of barbarians
8   who tell lies
    and raise their right hands to swear falsely.

9   O God, let me sing a new song to you
    and play for you on the ten-stringed lyre.

10 You give victory to your king,
    and rescue David, your servant.

11 Rescue me from Death's evil sword,
    and save me from the hands of barbarians who tell
        lies
    and raise their right hands to swear falsely.

12 May he bless our sons like seedlings,
    trained to grow straight from their youth.
    May he bless our daughters like pillars
    tapered for the building of a palace.

13 May our silos be full,
    packed from top to bottom.
    May our sheep lamb by the thousands,
    increasing to myriads in our pens.

14 May our cattle be well fed;
    may there be none that break out
    and none that stampede.
    May there be no disturbance in our pastures.

15 Happy the people who have these blessings.
    Happy the people whose God is Yahweh.

Psalm 145 (144)

A hymn of praise. Psalm 145 is an acrostic, each verse beginning with a different letter of the Hebrew alphabet in turn. The
second part of verse 13, here listed as "13a", is not found in the
present Hebrew text. It is supplied from the ancient versions.
The verse that should begin with the Hebrew letter "nun"
would fit into this spot, and undoubtedly the verse thus supplied by the ancient versions and the Dead Sea scrolls as well
was originally in the Hebrew text. The principal motif of this
hymn is the kingship of Yahweh and the qualities of his reign.
Many scholars regard this psalm as a late composition, but this
need not be the case. It may have been originally a hymn sung
at the fall festival.

1   *A hymn of praise of David.*

    I will praise you to high heaven,
    my God and my King;
    I will bless your Name to eternity and beyond.

2   Every day I will bless you:
    I will praise your Name to eternity and beyond.

3   Great is Yahweh and worthy of all praise;
    there is no comprehending his greatness.

4   One generation after another acclaims your deeds
    and relates your mighty works.

5   O Majestic Lord,
    they speak of your wonderful splendor
    and I ponder on your wonders.

6   O Mighty Lord, they speak of your awesome acts
    while I recount your famous deeds.

7   With enthusiasm they retell
    the record of all your abounding goodness;
    with joy they shout of your generosity.

8   Yahweh is kind and tender,
    slow to anger but quick in loving-kindness.

9   Yahweh's goodness is for everyone,
and his compassion extends to all his works.

10   All your works will praise you, Yahweh;
and all your devoted ones will bless you.

11   They speak of the splendor of your reign
and they tell of your power.

12   To all the children of men
they make your might known
and the majestic splendor of your kingdom.

13   Your kingdom is a kingdom for all eternity;
your dominion lasts age after age.

13a   Yahweh is faithful in all that he says,
kindly in all that he does.

14   Yahweh holds up all who are falling
and straightens up all who are bent over.

15   Every eye looks to you, Yahweh,
for you are the one who gives them their food
in due time.

16   You are the one who opens your hand
and fills every living thing with your favor.

17   All the ways of Yahweh are generous,
and all that he does is kindly.

18   Yahweh is close to all who call him;
he is close to all who call him with loyal hearts.

19   He fulfills the desires of all who reverence him;
he hears their cry for help and saves them.

20   Yahweh watches over all who love him,
but all the wicked he will destroy.

21   May my mouth speak the praise of Yahweh,
and may every living thing praise his holy Name
to eternity and beyond.

Psalm 146 (145)

Psalm 146 is a hymn of praise with some unusual features. It is a communal hymn but verse 1 is in the first person singular. Verses 2-10 are instructive in form, almost in the style of wisdom instructions found elsewhere in the Old Testament. In verses 7-10 the divine name "Yahweh" is repeated five times, giving a peculiarly intensive quality to the conclusion of this poem. It is not possible to date this psalm. Though most scholars regard it as post-exilic, there are elements in the psalm that seem very ancient.

1 Halleluia.

    Praise Yahweh, my soul!
    I will praise Yahweh as long as I live;

2 I will sing hymns to my God
    as long as I have life.

3 Put no trust in men of renown
    nor in any man at all
    because there is no salvation in them.

4 When their breath departs,
    they return to the dust,
    and on that day all their plans come to nothing.

5 Happy the man whose help is the God of Jacob
    and whose hope is God, Yahweh Most High.

6 He is the Maker of heaven and earth and sea
    and everything that is in them.
    He keeps his promises
    to those who have been wronged,

7 he defends the rights of the oppressed
    and provides the starving with food.

    Yahweh gives liberty to prisoners;
8 Yahweh gives sight to the blind;
    Yahweh straightens up all who are bent over.

    Yahweh loves the just;

9   Yahweh acts as guardian for the minorities.
Yahweh gives courage to widows and orphans,
but he undermines the regime of the wicked.

10   Yahweh will reign as king forever.
He will be your God, O Zion,
age after age.

Halleluia.

Psalm 147 (146)

What the Hebrew text treats as a single psalm was regarded by many ancient versions as two poems: verses 1-11 and 12-20. This division into two parts is probably correct, though both halves of Psalm 147 are hymns of praise. Moreover, both are probably post-exilic. There are certain resemblances in this psalm to Isaiah 40-55, and verse 2 speaks of the rebuilding of Jerusalem. Both parts of the psalm praise God for his special love for Israel and also for his providence as evidenced in nature.

1 Halleluia.

   How good it is to play music for our God!
   How pleasant to praise our Glorious One!

2 Yahweh rebuilds Jerusalem
   and reassembles the outcasts of Israel!

3 He heals the broken-hearted
   and bandages their wounds.

4 He decrees the number of the stars
   and assigns each of them its name.

5 Great is our Master and mighty his powers:
   there is no measuring his discerning intellect.

6 Yahweh gives courage
   to those who are destitute,
   he drives the wicked to the world below.

7 Sing your thanks to Yahweh;
   play music on the lyre for our God!

8 He makes the sky overcast with clouds;
   he prepares rain for the earth
   and makes grass to sprout on the mountains.

9 He feeds the cattle with their grain
   and the crows with what they gather.

10 He is not impressed by a horse's prowess
   nor entertained by any man's fleetness of foot.

11 Yahweh is pleased
   by men who reverence him
   and yearn for his unfailing love.

12 Acclaim Yahweh, O Jerusalem!
   O Zion, praise your God!

13 He has strengthened the bars on your gates
   and blessed your children who live inside.

14 He has surrounded you with prosperity
   and provided you with a surplus of the finest
      wheat.

15 He flings his thunder to the ground
   and his lightning-bolt races to the mountain peaks.

16 He spreads the snow like wool
   and strews the sparkling frost like ashes.

17 He hurls hailstones down like splinters,
   and who can survive such cold?

18 He issues an order and the thaw begins;
   he lets the breeze blow
   and the water starts to flow.

19 He reveals his word to Jacob,
   his laws and his decisions to Israel.

20 He has not done this for any other nation,
   nor has he informed others of his decisions.

Halleluia.

Psalm 148

A hymn of praise. The psalm falls into three distinct parts. Verses 1-6 address all the beings of heaven. Verse 7 is a brief nod to the nether-world. All the creatures of the earth are called upon to render their praise in verses 8-14, with special emphasis falling upon Israel itself. No date can be assigned to this hymn but it is interesting to note that it has ancient Egyptian counterparts, as well as relatively late ones in the Old Testament itself, such as Job 38 and Daniel 4:52ff.

1 Halleluia.

    Praise Yahweh from the heavens!
    Praise him from the vault of highest heaven!

2 Praise him, all his angels!
    Praise him, all his armies of angels!

3 Praise him, sun and moon!
    Praise him, stars of morning!

4 Praise him, heavens beyond the heavens!
    Praise him, waters beyond the heavens!

5 Let them praise the name of Yahweh
    because at his command they were created.

6 He assigned them their places forever and ever
    by making a decree which never will be repealed.

7 Praise Yahweh from the earth below!
    Dragons and primeval oceans,

8 fire and smoke, hail and snow,
    violent winds that obey his commands;

9 mountains and every height,
    fruit trees and every forest,

10 every animal, wild and tame,
    reptiles and birds that fly;

11 kings of the earth and every people,
    officials and every tribe of the earth;

12 the best of the youth and maidens too,
    elders and young people as well:

13 let them praise the name of Yahweh,
    because his name alone is glorious;
    his splendor surpasses earth and sky,

14 but he gives prosperity to his people.
    Praise from all who are devoted to him,
    from the sons of Israel,
    the people who are close to him!

    Halleluia.

Psalm 149

A hymn of praise. The rather simple first appearance of Psalm 149 belies a host of difficulties and scholars have been sharply divided over its place in Israel's life as well as the time of its origin. Only on the mysteriousness of the meaning behind this hymn are they agreed. The setting in which this poem was used may have been a liturgy for the new year festival, in which a cultic ritual portrayed the conquest of the world by the Lord and his people. On the other hand it may have been a true war song, a prayer for victory and an interpretation of the holy war as being God's own battle. Verses 1-4 are a call to praise. Verses 5-9 seem to be a description of a sabre dance in which the people are encouraged to participate by their cries. The enemies will be led away in a triumph and thus the purpose of God in the world will be brought about.

1 Halleluia.

> Sing a new song to Yahweh!
> Sing his praise in the assembly of his faithful!

2 Let Israel be glad in its supreme maker;
let the sons of Zion rejoice with their king!

3 Let them praise his name with a dance;
let them sing to him with drum and harp!

4 Indeed, Yahweh is pleased with his people;
he adorns his poor with the ornaments of
salvation.

5 Let his faithful dance for joy
because of their Glorious One!
From their seats let them cry out for gladness!

6 Let high praises of God come from their throats!
Let two-edged swords be in their hands

7 to accomplish vengeance on the nations,
retaliation against the peoples;

8 to manacle their kings with chains,
their men of renown with iron shackles;

9 to carry out on them the prescribed verdict!
   This is an honor reserved for all those devoted to
   him.

   Halleluia.

Psalm 150

The first four books of the psalter are concluded with brief
doxologies. Psalm 150 serves as a doxology for the whole
psalter. It is a grand hymn of praise drawing a whole liturgical
orchestra into the acclaim of God. The imperative verb
"Praise!" is ten times repeated in this psalm; this tenfold
repetition may of course be coincidental, but it may be a
response to the ten words of creation in the beginning or it may
correspond to the ten commandments. The "sanctuary" of
verse 1 is apparently the heavenly palace, and the praise of
creation that follows is thus drawn into the heavenly liturgy.

1 Halleluia.

   Praise God in his sanctuary!
   Praise him under the dome of his palace!

2 Praise him for his mighty power!
   Praise him for his immeasurable greatness!

3 Praise him with trumpet flourishes!
   Praise him with harp and lyre!

4 Praise him with drum and dance!
   Praise him with strings and flute!

5 Praise him with cymbals that clash!
   Praise him with cymbals that ring!

6 Everything that has breath:
   Praise Yahweh!

   Halleluia.